How We Eat

How We Eat

Appetite, Culture, and the Psychology of Food

LEON RAPPOPORT, PH.D.

ECW PRESS

Published by ECW PRESS
2120 Queen Street East, Suite 200, Toronto, Ontario, Canada M4E 1E2

NATIONAL LIBRARY OF CANADA CATALOGUING IN PUBLICATION DATA

Rappoport, Leon
How we eat: appetite, culture, and the psychology of food / Leon Rappoport
ISBN 1-55022-563-4
1. Food habits—History. 2. Food habits—Psychological aspects. I. Title.
GT2860.R36 2003   394.1'09   C2002-905418-4

Acquisition editor: Emma McKay
Copy editor: Judy Phillips
Design and typesetting: Yolande Martel
Production: Emma McKay
Printing: Transcontinental
Cover design: Guylaine Regimbald – SOLO DESIGN
Front cover illustration: John Martin

This book is set in Electra

The publication of *How We Eat: Appetite, Culture, and the Psychology of Food*
has been generously supported by the Canada Council, by the Government of
Ontario through the Ontario Media Development Corporation's Ontario Book
Initiative, by the Ontario Arts Council, and by the Government of Canada
through the Book Publishing Industry Development Program. Canada

DISTRIBUTION

CANADA: Jaguar Book Group, 100 Armstrong Avenue,
Georgetown, Ontario L7G 5S4

UNITED STATES: Independent Publishers Group, 814 North Franklin Street,
Chicago, Illinois 60610

EUROPE: Turnaround Publisher Services, Unit 3, Olympia Trading Estate,
Coburg Road, Wood Green, London N2Z 6T2

AUSTRALIA AND NEW ZEALAND: Wakefield Press, 1 The Parade West
(BOX 2266), Kent Town, South Australia 5071

PRINTED AND BOUND IN CANADA

ECW PRESS
ecwpress.com

*To Lula Francis and in memory
of her Uncle Paul*

Contents

Acknowledgments

WHEN IT COMES TO FOOD and eating habits, practically everyone has something interesting to say. But since the list of all those colleagues, students, friends, and family members who in one way or another contributed toward the development of this book could approximate a small telephone directory, I can single out only a few for special thanks.

The idea that food carries profound social-psychological meanings, and that our eating behaviors represent important ways of our "being in the world," first emerged from work I was doing on psychological aspects of the Holocaust with my friend and colleague George M. Kren. It was clear to both of us that starvation was a major factor allowing the Nazis to dehumanize many of their victims. As a historian of modern European culture, George was fully aware of both the symbolic and the concrete significance of food in human affairs, and he offered important perspectives on the contents of this book.

I am also grateful to Joe Amato, a leading historian of Midwestern American culture, for his encouragement and helpful critical reading of the draft manuscript. Some of the research findings noted in the book grew out of discussions with my colleagues Ron Downey and George Peters. Over several years, we conducted a series of studies focused on the various ways different people (young and old, men and women) think about food and negotiate their desires for tastiness, health, and convenience. Later joined by Lin Huff-Corzine, our research group became a major source of support for the book project. I am indebted to all of them, particularly Ron Downey, who has seen it all the way through with me.

Many of the ideas discussed in chapter 4 were developed in collaboration with Julio Angulo when he was completing his graduate studies with me. Originally from Chile, Julio has traveled widely and has a strong sense of the extent to which food and cuisine can be a vehicle conveying social and political ideologies. This is also true of my friend Erika Apfelbaum, a French social psychologist based at the National Center for Social Research in Paris. We met during one of her visits to the U.S. and discovered that we had almost identical views on the meanings of food in daily life, including that it was generally ignored by most social scientists. Much of the material examined in this book is based on the work we did together when I was able to spend part of a sabbatical in Paris. Her insights and belief in the importance of the project have been invaluable.

A Half-Baked Notion

I T HAS BEEN SAID so many times in so many ways by so many scholars and cuisine authorities as to be a cliché: eating is as much or more a matter of the mind as it is of the body. Yet if you take this seriously enough to look beyond superficial discussions of the mind–body connection in popular magazines and dieting books, you don't find much readily accessible information about what the cliché really means. Instead, what you see are mainly descriptions of gimmicks and quick fixes aimed at people trying to manage their appetite and anxiety issues.

After providing more or less lip service to the importance of "mind" (read "willpower"), most of this material suggests that if you can't (a) chew each mouthful twenty or thirty times, (b) drink three glasses of water before each meal, (c) take four deep breaths between each bite, (d) visualize the roll of fat around your middle or the clumps of cholesterol in your arteries, and so forth, to control your consumption, there is always the local acupuncturist ready to manipulate your appetite centers, or better, the money-back-if-it-doesn't-work hypnotist.

It must be acknowledged, of course, that some of the gimmicks work some of the time for some people. But in any case, why should we bother about the mind–body significance of food? The wide and deep range of social, emotional, and biological implications of our eating behaviors hardly ever come up in daily life, so why should anyone take time to examine them? This is not an easy question to answer because the pathways that lead any of us toward food as a subject for serious thought or study vary across an immense spectrum of experience. At the positive end are those who from childhood onward were captivated by the magical joys of eating—magical in the sense that the delicious food treats of their childhood could immediately overwhelm moments of injury or sadness with visceral pleasure. According to recent biographies, cuisine experts such as Julia Child and M.F.K. Fisher, who were raised in comfortable upper-middle-class families, probably began this way. Their adult concerns with food might be understood as a search for the keys to the magical kingdom of culinary delights, where recipes are incantations, cooking is alchemy, and efforts to find a great cuisine or restaurant are like quests for a Holy Grail.

At the negative end of the spectrum are those unfortunates for whom food, sometimes from the beginning of childhood, has been a problem, often a threatening source of anxiety. In her text on the psychology of eating and drinking, psychologist A.W. Logue explains that her professional work on the subject may stem from the fact that she had rigid food aversions as far back as she can remember, and that for much of her early childhood she survived mostly on milk and bread. Gandhi's autobiography, on the other hand, explains that he first became sensitized not only to the personal significance of his eating habits but also to the social and cultural importance of food when, upon his arrival in England as a young law student, he was pressured to abandon his vegetarian diet.

Most of us fall somewhere between these extremes, generally accepting the foods of our culture or subculture without much thought. The exception might be during childhood and adolescence, when a novel, "foreign" dish occasionally confronts us as a frightening enigma. A case in point is my own experience as a twelve-year-old Boy Scout, when I first violated the laws that define kosher foods by tasting ham and bacon, half expecting to be struck down by an Orthodox Jewish thunderbolt, or at least a major stomach ache. But I got away clean and went on to become a typically omnivorous teenager, primarily concerned with quantity, not quality. This continued more or less unchanged until I stumbled unwittingly into the profound implications of food while doing research on the Holocaust and, at about the same time, learning the practices of yoga and Zen Buddhist meditation.

These were my main professional and personal projects from about age forty to fifty. The former was a scholarly research effort to unravel the historical and psychological factors that made the Holocaust possible. The latter was an exploration of unusual, sometimes painful, mental and physical states, carried out under the instruction of Zen master Dainin Katagiri. Both projects involved years of demanding work and occasional bafflement. They also brought rewarding insights, and always a sense of working toward a deeper grasp of human behavior. I never imagined that the two projects might ultimately converge, and then dissolve, into something so prosaic as food! Yet that's what happened as I began to see that, beneath the horrors of Holocaust testimony and the dramatic accounts of Zen enlightenments, there was a truth of startling simplicity—namely that, among other things, both point to the body as the inescapable source of our human condition. Even if it were not so prominent as it is in the Holocaust and Zen literatures, consideration of the body would lead inevitably to reflection on the significance of food in shaping our existential condition. But food *is* a central theme in Holocaust research and Zen philosophy. Without exception, Holocaust victim and survivor accounts show that starvation led rapidly to demoralization and even dehumanization.

Holocaust survivor Elie Cohen noted that in the camps "food was a very favorite topic of conversation. The prisoners would go 'dining out' together and exchange recipes for special dishes." Some of them referred to these conversations as "culinary dry screwing." For Primo Levi, who wrote eloquently about his imprisonment in Auschwitz, the worst of the starvation experiences were the dreams. He could tell when his fellow prisoners were dreaming of eating by the way they worked their jaws and licked their lips. In his own dreams, he could smell desirable items and feel them on his lips.

These accounts, and countless others that could be cited, require little elaboration. Without an adequate diet, a person's behavior deteriorates to a primal level, and basic dimensions of human dignity may be lost. Indeed, many prisoners in the Nazi camps reached such a dehumanized state that they were referred to by other prisoners as *musselmanner*, or zombies.

The other side of my path toward food involved yoga and Zen practices. Either by chance or some odd twist of fate, just as my work on the Holocaust was revealing the dehumanizing effects of starvation, I was also learning that food can be a powerful spiritual medium leading to an enhanced sense of one's humanity. That is, Zen Buddhist teachings emphasize the importance of appreciating food consumption as concrete evidence of our unity with nature. This may be experienced as an aesthetic experience during intensive meditation retreats, when for several days all food is served and eaten in silence, except for ceremonial procedures that include group chanting ("Innumerable labors have brought us this food, we should know how it comes to us . . ."). The elaborate etiquette of serving and receiving is designed to promote awareness of eating as an act of communion with all beings. Such a holy view of food is present to some extent in all religions, but in Zen it has become an integral part of the daily practice of "mindfulness of mind."

The Holocaust work and Zen practices started me ruminating about the psychological significance of food, and several incidental events led me further into the subject. Early on was an occasion at a colleague's home. We were examining a collection of gruesome photographs of Holocaust victims when he was called to the telephone. Wanting a change of pace while I waited, I picked up a gourmet magazine that was lying on his coffee table. Glancing through the pictures of blackened red fish, roast beef, paella, and legs of lamb, I suddenly realized that this was no less a pornography than the photos of skeletal Nazi victims. Both were similar in their appeal to visual sensations or, as the Old Testament has it, "the lust of the eye."

Another, more substantial, incident occurred when I was at a conference in New York on the significance of dialectical philosophy for psychology. At the first lunch break, my group fell into lively debate on where to eat. Choosing from the various cuisines available in nearby restaurants evoked equal if not greater arguments than our discussions of abstract philosophy. This is not that unusual: a primary concern of people at most professional meetings is where to eat, what to eat, and with whom to eat. But now it struck me that we were acting out one of the principles of dialectical thought that we had earlier been trying to clarify: the idea that many activities lead to their own contradictions. In this instance, the dialectic of digestion would ensure that, no matter what we ate for lunch, it would ultimately be transformed into shit. Furthermore, any traditional Marxist would add that, in seeking an unusual cuisine, we were subordinating the use value (nutrition) of our lunch to its exchange value (style). Excited by this discovery of the contradiction between our theory and practice, I tried to express it to one of my colleagues, who listened, smiled tolerantly, and said, "Ah, yes, I see, the Marxist approach to cuisine: sauces are the opium of the taste buds." A perfect put-down, and I still wonder if he invented it on the spot.

During this time, too, I began looking into the seemingly infinite literature on food: the historical, anthropological, sociological, philosophical, physiological, psychological, and metaphysical approaches to the meanings of food and ways of eating. The amount of material available was daunting, and no comfort was to be found when I mentioned my growing interest in food to colleagues. Most of their responses varied from amused dismissal in the form of puns ("A half-baked notion" and "You don't expect me to swallow that?") to interested bewilderment ("What exactly do you want to know about food?" and "Isn't the study of foodways a subject for anthropologists?"). The humorous remarks were easy enough to tolerate, but the questions about what I was after were more trouble-some because I had no simple answers.

Of course, there are the obvious generalizations about the social-psychological uses of food. Virtually all distinct cultural, ethnic, and national groups define themselves, and tend to denigrate others, by asserting the superiority of the foods that represent their social and moral values. What "we" eat is good, what "they" eat is bad. And apart from the meanings associated with specific foods, the ways of preparing and eating them also involve cultural, ethnic, and social class prejudices. At the individual level, eating habits can be quite revealing of person-ality. The ways we relate to food (smash and grab versus picky and pokey, and everything in-between) can reveal a great deal about how we see ourselves and relate with others. These commonsense observations were good enough to spar with in conversations but are really no more than interesting fragments in search of a central thesis. It took me another few years to realize that, where the meanings of food are concerned, the *absence* of a central thesis *is* the central thesis.

Since I could not blitz the subject matter with a penetrating thesis, the only option was to envelop it by probing on a broad front. But as I continued to scout the scholarly and popular literatures, I found that, like some character in a *Star Trek* scenario, instead of me enveloping that novel world of food meanings and eating behaviors, it was enveloping me. And all I could do was create a paper trail about the intriguing topics I was encountering: Claude Lévi-Strauss's theory of cuisine; Norbert Elias's study of the evolution of table manners; the development of new food products; the controversial interpre-tations of cannibalism, eating disorders, advertising tactics, and health-food metaphysics; the sociocultural histories of sugar, potatoes, corn, fast foods, French cuisine, military field rations; and so on. I lost myself in the extraordinary variety of material, and after a few years I no longer worried about it. I simply gathered my notes into an eclectic archive.

While wandering in this wilderness as a hunter-gatherer of intellectual nuggets, however, I found that, apart from the puns and questions about what I was up to, almost everyone—from first-year college student to tenured professor—wanted to know more about the topic. Often they would describe, unsolicited, some of their own experiences with food. One of the first occurrences of this was during a visit with the noted Gestalt theorist Fritz Heider. Responding to my interest in the psychological meanings of food, he said it brought back a childhood memory of his eccentric aunt. She would serve sliced tomatoes sprinkled with salt as a salad, and sliced tomatoes sprinkled with sugar as a dessert. A wonderful example, we thought, of one of the principles of Gestalt theory, whereby our perception of an object can be radically changed if some detail of the object is altered.

Curiously, many of the food experiences people mention relate to either their childhood or to their own children. The childhood memories are often of being forced to eat disliked foods (usually liver or hot cereals) or of the opposite, such as the blissful pleasures of eating freshly baked cookies in Grandma's kitchen. Adult memories, on the other hand, frequently relate to the tricks and schemes employed to get children to eat healthy foods. When feeding my own children their mashed baby foods, for example, I could get them to take a spoonful of the vegetables by topping it off with a veneer of the fruit.

Unfortunately, they would catch on pretty quickly and spit it back at me.

Then there was the story I heard from a prominent psychologist about her daughter who, from about ages five to ten, refused to eat anything in the morning except her mother's French toast. And that of the divorced father raising two teenagers, who explained that his children would only nibble at the hearty breakfasts he made for them each morning, but he kept it up anyway to show them he cared. What became clear from these and countless other stories is that, although one would never know it from the psychology textbooks, which give little or no attention to everyday food experiences, the social-emotional functions and uses of food in daily life are ubiquitous. Indeed, there is hardly any significant social activity or emotional state to which food is irrelevant, and there are many, such as parent–child relationships, to which it is central. Why, then, have food behaviors not been a major area of study in the field of psychology?

There are a number of reasons for this, but three explanations stand out. First and most apparent is the division of labor in the social sciences: almost everything related to the social and cultural significance of food has traditionally been assigned to anthropology. But while anthropologists have provided vast material on the important social functions of food, particularly the variations among many "primitive" societies, they have generally not been concerned with psychological factors. When Margaret Mead was in charge of a U.S. government program to examine American food habits during World War II, she recognized this problem and appointed the social psychologist Kurt Lewin as her primary investigator. His research demonstrating that housewives of the 1940s were the gatekeepers of the American diet, and that their attitudes toward food were resistant to change but could be manipulated by group pressure, has become a classic in the literature of social psychology and nutrition science.

The second explanation is that, with a few exceptions such as Lewin (and he studied food behaviors for only a few years), psychologists have been interested in food primarily from the standpoint of either psychobiology—the sensory and neural processes related to taste, obesity, and alcoholism—or psychopathology—the social-emotional problems associated with anorexia and bulimia.

Finally, and most importantly, food has not been seen as a central problem in psychology, sociology, or the other social sciences (anthropology has traditionally put more emphasis on toilet training and kinship systems) because it did not receive much attention from influential social theorists. One searches in vain through the major theoretical writings of modernity— Karl Marx, Sigmund Freud, B.F. Skinner, Talcott Parsons, Jean Piaget, Margaret Mead, and so on—for any serious consideration of food behavior. It was generally taken for granted as a fact of life, worthy of attention only when symptomatic of some other, more significant, problem. In general, then, although my informal conversations and observations clearly indicated that food carries important psychological meanings, relevant source material was scarce and scattered across the social sciences.

The situation began to change in the 1980s because of medical findings that emphasized the significance of diet to health, and because of rising interest in the new field of health psychology. Studies of food behaviors began to gain a much higher academic status. The first college textbook on the psychology of food was published in 1986. Meanwhile, increasing concern with food pathologies and the dietary issues associated with cancer, heart disease, and diabetes encouraged research. But most of this activity still had little to do with the everyday meanings of food.

My pursuit of this topic accelerated after meeting Erika Apfelbaum, a French psychologist. When my interest in food came up in conversation, she understood it immediately and surprised me with some striking observations of her own. Her remark that "Americans eat with their eyes, but the French eat with their noses" moved us directly into a long discussion of cultural differences rooted in the food experiences of children. At the same time, Julio Angulo, a doctoral candidate who participated in some of the discussions with Apfelbaum, also became interested in this topic. Having grown up in Chile and studied in California before moving to the U.S. Midwest, Angulo had a strong sense of the different attitudes Latinos and North Americans have toward food. The thesis project he proceeded to work on with me focused on the concept of food ideologies. This turned out to be something of a breakthrough study because it showed that belief systems about food could be analyzed using many of the same criteria applied to political ideologies. And whether prescribed in the texts of nutrition scientists or the alternative texts of vegetarians, dietary ideologies also appeared to reflect attitudes toward the world in general. In short, Angulo's analysis provided convincing evidence that the French writer and gourmet Anthelme Brillat-Savarin was quite correct in his famous observation of 1825: "Tell me what you eat and I will tell you what you are."

Soon afterward, I spent two months in Paris mapping out with Apfelbaum a general plan for the study of food meanings. There is no better place to think about questions of food and be reassured that they are important. Every city park and tourist attraction is dotted with the carts of vendors selling sandwiches or snacks, and every residential area has its share of bakeries, groceries, and delicatessens, often with tempting sidewalk displays. Nor can one avoid the open-air markets that spring up overnight in different districts or the ever-present cafés, with seemingly permanent cadres of customers drinking and eating at sidewalk tables. It didn't take long for the city to begin to feel like a huge, multifaceted eating emporium. After about a month, I thought to epitomize this with the aphorism "You know you've adapted to Paris when the first thing you think of upon getting up in the morning is where you'll be having lunch." In fact, morning work sessions with Apfelbaum were usually followed by a "field trip" to an affordable working-class restaurant for lunch. These places were remarkable. To enter what looks like an overcrowded bar and be led down a narrow hallway by a husky *patronne* who looks and sounds like Maurice Chevalier in drag and then to be seated at a table six inches away from total strangers—who might or might not look up and nod before going on with their meal—took getting used to.

It was an instructive routine, marred only by the fact that it led to a dead end because it could not accommodate certain issues, such as acquired tastes. Why is it, for example, that people come to enjoy certain items, such as black coffee, olives, hot peppers, or martinis, which they initially disliked? And how come certain items, such as bagels, pizza, and croissants, migrate from their culture of origin and attain world-class status?

There was also the vexing problem of cause and effect: that food preferences can be analyzed convincingly as both a cause and a consequence of social or emotional processes. In the end, such knotty issues overwhelmed our project. We could not formulate any set of general principles able to stand up under the burden of important exceptions. I left Paris with about sixty pages of notes on the various meanings of food, one of which—the prevalence of food metaphors and aphorisms in everyday speech—seemed perfectly representative of our situation: we had bitten off more than we could chew.

All my notes eventually led to the development of three central ideas about the meanings of food that could provide a foundation for further work. First was the theme, based primarily on the work of Claude Lévi-Strauss, that our food behaviors serve as a largely unacknowledged bridge between the given world of nature and the made world of culture. Lévi-Strauss was referring here to the little magic acts we carry out when we transform the raw goods of nature into the cooked items of cuisine. Second was the point that, in general, most people, popular food writers and culture critics included, are reluctant to look closely at the ways in which our food habits bind us to the "tooth and claw" world of nature—probably because it's too bloody. And this also applies to many prominent social theorists. As I suggested in a 1987 article on the subject, no matter what other differences have existed between them, nothing except time or money has ever prevented dedicated Marxists or Freudians, humanists or hard scientists, from enjoying the taken-for-granted pleasures of cuisine. Critical thinking apparently stops at the dinner table. And third was the idea that food behaviors have taken on an ambiguous status in much of the world, as traditional dietary practices have been undermined by the new products, cooking technologies, and other changes associated with modernization. The evidence for this is all too obvious. In North America today, and much of the rest of the world too, hardly any parents feed their children the same things they ate when *they* were children.

Based on these ideas, and with the help of a few sympathetic colleagues, I began a series of research studies designed to investigate how people think and feel about their food preferences and eating habits. Our initial surveys and interviews showed that, while pleasurable (good-tasting) foods were generally thought to be unhealthy, pleasure was, nevertheless, the most important criterion in most people's food choices; health was secondary. Elderly women were the most likely to focus on the health factor. People largely ignored symbolic or metaphysical meanings of food except to the extent that they associated certain foods with traditional holidays such as Thanksgiving and Christmas. On the other hand, in addition to the criteria of pleasure and health, people often mentioned convenience: some foods were primarily meaningful because they were easy to get or prepare. It was also in this context that we first encountered the macaroni-and-cheese phenomenon — namely that, particularly among younger people, it is a popular comfort food seen as pleasurable, healthy, and extremely convenient.

While this work was going forward, I was trying to figure out how the diverse psychological meanings of food could be brought together in a coherent book. It had seemed to me for some time that the very diversity and complexity that made the social and emotional meanings of food such an interesting problem also ensured its impregnability to analysis. But then I began to see the problem differently. What happened was analogous to the change in perception that occurs when one realizes that staring at clumps of trees cannot lead to an understanding of the forest. Rather than continuing to puzzle out some sort of scheme that would embrace all or most aspects of food behavior, I became increasingly preoccupied with the sheer diversity. In one of our survey studies, for example, approximately three hundred people, many of them members of the same families, listed what they had eaten for breakfast. The range of responses was huge. No two were exactly alike, and some of the differences were extreme, involving everything from candy bars to leftover pizza, peanut butter on toast, hot water, diet drinks, yogurt, fruits, vegetables, and variations on the conventional breakfasts of eggs and cereals.

Yet our sample was from a relatively stable, homogeneous community in the U.S. Midwest. The differences within it are pale compared with what might be found in Chicago or Los Angeles. Certainly the food world of any person or group has firm cultural boundaries—you don't find yak butter or whale steak in most North American supermarkets—but within the boundaries defining our food world, almost anything goes. Indeed, the more closely one examines food habits, the more striking are the differences between individuals related to demographic categories (age, gender, education, income), physiology (body weight, metabolism, general health), and psychological factors (personal values, family traditions, emotional states), not to mention the possible combinations of all these categories. Even people who appear quite similar to each other in all these categories—brother and sisters close to the same age who grew up together—typically develop very different food habits.

Such observations eventually led me to a new perspective. After thinking for years that the problem was how to deal with a world of food meanings, it now seemed to me that what one had to deal with was not a *world* but a *universe* of many worlds, each with its own internal dynamics. Instead of trying to find order in the endless diversity, one had to see that the diversity *is* the order, and then get on with mapping its psychological implications. Viewed in this light, the problems I had been seeing as roadblocks began to look like signposts showing the way to go forward. The results are offered, *bon appétit*, in the following chapters.

CHAPTER 1

From Myths to MacAttacks

THERE IS AN EMBARRASSING emperor's-new-clothes question about food behaviors that sooner or later imposes itself
on anyone who takes this subject seriously: what *is* food? The
question comes up partly from both research and common
experiences showing that items considered to be good food, or
even special delicacies in one group, culture, or subculture,
are considered by others to be unfit for human consumption.
It is often found more dramatically in the memoirs of world
travelers and explorers. In *The Oregon Trail,* for example,
Frances Parkman describes in striking detail the first time he ate
a puppy dog. He was a guest in an Indian lodge at Fort Laramie
when his host's oldest wife entered, carrying a tomahawk:
"I had observed sometime before a litter of well grown black
puppies, comfortably nestled among some buffalo-robes at one
side; but this newcomer speedily disturbed their enjoyment;
for seizing one of them by the hind paw, she dragged him out,
and carrying him to the entrance of the lodge, hammered him
on the head till she killed him. Conscious to what this preparation tended, I looked through a hole in the back of the lodge
to see the next step of the process. The squaw, holding the
puppy by the legs, was swinging him to and fro through the

blaze of a fire, until the hair was singed off. This done, she unsheathed her knife and cut him into small pieces, which she dropped into a kettle to boil. In a few moments a large wooden dish was set before us, filled with this delicate preparation. A dog feast is the greatest compliment a Dacotah can offer to his guest; and knowing that to refuse eating would be an affront, we attacked the little dog and devoured him before the eyes of his unconscious parent."

There is no mistaking Parkman's studied sense of repulsion at this scene. It was all the more impressive, therefore, to discover in *Undaunted Courage,* Steven Ambrose's account of the 1804 Lewis and Clark expedition from St. Louis to the Columbia River, quotations from the journal of Meriwether Lewis indicating that he and his men had acquired a taste for dog meat and preferred it to the game and horse meat they often lived on.

My own experiences with the cultural relativism of cuisine have been relatively trivial. While I was stationed in Germany in 1955, my wife bought some corn on the cob at the army commissary. When our German landlady happened to see it, she made a face, calling it "pig food." Several years later, the shoe was on the other foot: while we were on a research fellowship in Oslo, a Norwegian colleague invited us to a traditional holiday meal of *ludefisk* (boiled dried cod), which we were just barely able to get down. My wife threw it all up when we got home. The moral of the story is that the body does not swallow cultural relativism as easily as the mind.

For their part, nutrition experts and other authorities never seem to bother much with the question of just what *is* food; they are apparently content with the commonsense notion that food is simply the stuff that people eat, while pointing out that the stuff most of us are eating is not very healthy. There's nothing terribly wrong with this, except that, when you look in the dictionary, the definitions of food turn out to be a bit problematic. According to the 1981 edition of *Webster's Unabridged Dictionary*, food is "material consisting of carbohydrates, fats, proteins and supplementary substances (as minerals, vitamins) that is taken or absorbed into the body of an animal in order to sustain growth, repair, and all vital processes and to furnish energy for all activity of the organism." This is pretty straightforward and properly scientistic, but the abstract language has slightly sinister overtones. There is nothing in it, after all, that would preclude having the juicier parts of Aunt Sophie or Felix the cat for lunch. And the subordinate dictionary description tends to confirm this implication: ". . . esp., parts of the bodies of animals and plants consumed by animals."

This line of thought about food was taken to its ultimate extreme by Ernest Becker. In *The Denial of Death*, he discusses the human condition as being a function of "appetite and ingenuity." And he refers to all animal life on our planet as a "gory spectacle" in which organisms are constantly struggling to feed on each other, on the one hand chewing up any flesh they can get hold of, and on the other hand leaving behind a trail of "fuming waste excrement." A similar but less embellished view was offered by Ambrose Bierce in *The Devil's Dictionary*. He defined "edible" as "Good to eat, and wholesome to digest, as a worm to a toad, a toad to a snake, a snake to a pig, a pig to a man, and a man to a worm."

The point at issue here is simply that a good case can be made for the argument that, where human eating habits are concerned, "anything goes." But, of course, in practice it doesn't; we may be omnivorous, but we do draw the line here and there. Just where we draw the line varies between societies, as well as between cultural groups and individuals within any society; the diverse meanings of food can be appreciated simply by scanning regional, social class, and ethnic differences in cuisine. But it becomes painfully clear in hardship situations when food is in short supply. In his book on the sociology of cooking, *Cooking, Cuisine and Class,* Jack Goody describes an incident that occurred while he was a prisoner of war during World War II. The prisoners were always hungry, and although they lived on limited rations and Red Cross parcels, they would nevertheless scrounge and save up food items so they could celebrate special occasions with a hearty meal. One Christmas, Goody and a friend were invited to a meal prepared by other prisoners. It consisted of an anonymous but tasty meat stew. Goody thought the prisoners had bribed one of the guards to bring in a rabbit but, after the meal was over, was told by his proud host that the stew was made of cat meat. Instead of feeling disturbed at the news that he had just been guilty of what he called "quasi cannibalism," Goody congratulated his host for having found a new way to supplement their diet. He then returned to his own quarters and suggested to those he lived with that they try to get a cat for *their* Christmas dinner. They were appalled at the idea and refused to have anything to do with it.

Another prisoner of war, Bernard Clavell (who would become the best-selling author of *Shogun* and other novels) was held by the Japanese during World War II. His *roman à clef* about life in the camp, *King Rat,* describes a systematic trade in the rats that prisoners killed and ate. By an odd coincidence—what Jungian theorists might call a "synchronicity"—I recently found that there is at least one place in the world where cooked rats are a restaurant specialty. An article by an American journalist working in China describes restaurants in the village of Luogang where customers can browse through a selection of caged rats and choose the ones they wish to have killed and cooked for their dinners. These restaurants also offer a range of cats and snakes.

Violations of our conventional food norms or taboos do not stop at household pets or rodents. In severe starvation situations, especially when prolonged suffering or abuse has reduced people to a state of demoralization, cannibalism may occur. In the U.S., there is the well-known story of pioneers in the Donner party wagon train, some of whom turned to eating body parts of their dead companions when snowbound in the mountains of California. Less well known but more horrific is the cannibalism that set in among some of the half million Germans and Italians captured by the Soviet army after the battle for Stalingrad in 1943. According to the testimony of survivors gathered by the historian William Craig, the Soviets could not cope with this massive number of prisoners, so the prisoners were sent on forced marches in freezing weather and herded together in improvised camps with little or no food or shelter. Under these conditions, a few of the prisoners, crazed by hunger and cold, turned to cannibalism. At first, the cannibals took only the arms or legs of the dead, eating them raw, but later they formed groups and attacked the bodies of men who were not yet dead. The situation became so horrific that other prisoners organized vigilante squads to wipe out the cannibals.

Our visceral revulsion at stories of people consuming their pets, or worse, human flesh, is powerful evidence of the degree to which we internalize food norms. Rather than violate these norms, many people will accept death. And our response to the opposite extreme of voluntary starvation offers similarly strong evidence for the power of socially conditioned food norms. Just as cannibalism poses a frightening threat to any group in which it occurs—if this taboo can be violated, nothing is safe!—so too does the deliberate renunciation of food, as in a hunger strike or in the pathology of anorexia. Our visceral reactions to this may be less intense than those triggered by cannibalism, but insofar as people deliberately reject food, they are rejecting a fundamental shared value of the community. And by doing so, they threaten the ties that hold that community together. Conversely, it is through the sharing of food that people demonstrate their support and acceptance of communal ties. One of the unmistakable and often unconscious tactics of teenagers in Western society who are trying to establish a sense of identity apart from their parents frequently is played out at the dinner table when they begin to reject or criticize familiar family food items. If we are indeed what we eat, then what we refuse to eat, we are not! The stubborn refusal of food can be a profound negation. It is not surprising, therefore, that hunger strikers will be force fed, anorexics forced into therapy, and even dying elderly patients trying to refuse food to end their suffering fed intravenously.

When viewed in this context, food can also begin to be understood as a primary medium for the exercise of social power. Consider, for a moment, the child facing an unfamiliar food for the first time, or an adult encountering a strange cuisine. If they are to satisfy their hunger and the demands of the social situation, which usually include some pressure to conform, they must endure the anxiety of tasting and swallowing an uncertain, perhaps alien and therefore threatening, substance. Children frequently respond with spontaneous resistance by spitting things out. Most adults, however, will typically pretend enjoyment even if their visceral reactions are negative, lest they offend their hosts. The procedures and instruments by which a novel food must be eaten can evoke a similar experience of intimidation. Many of us have suffered embarrassed frustration before our first lobster, artichoke, or effort to eat with chopsticks. (And then, of course, once we have mastered the required skills, we usually look down on the struggling novice with amused superiority.) Ultimately, the hungry person has little or no recourse against the forms of social control that may be imposed as a condition against satisfying that hunger. Food can be such an effective vehicle of social control that it is routinely used as the chief reward or reinforcer when training our dogs, cats, and, too often, children.

Apart from the limits set by the two "forbidden" extremes of cannibalism and voluntary starvation, the definitions and meanings of acceptable food items vary across a wide range of cultural practices. At bottom, however, there is a general psychological dynamic, or call it simply a fundamental type of magical thinking, that characterizes the way different organic materials have come to be accepted as edible. Anthropological evidence shows that, in all primitive human groups, seasonal variations in plant life and animal behaviors were thought to be governed by mysterious forces under the full or partial control of sundry gods, goddesses, and spirits. And according to all the myths and rituals associated with primitive human food activities, the whims, wishes, and arbitrary actions of these metaphysical beings dictated both the availability of certain plants or animals and their suitability for human consumption.

Virtually all the basic foods we eat today—the cereal grains, fruits, vegetables, meats, and fishes—have a mythic, sacred pedigree. Sacred because, for our primitive ancestors, to consume something either given by, or stolen from, the gods was to participate in the cosmic mysteries controlled by those gods. As anthropologists have noted, for many primitives, eating is a "communion with the sacred." The names of many staple foods carry traces of their metaphysical origin myths. The term "cereals," for example, is derived from the Greek myth of the goddess Ceres, whose daughter, Persephone, was stolen by Pluto, god of the underworld, and required to sleep with him beneath the earth each winter. As Ceres searched the underworld for her daughter, she scattered behind her gifts in the form of seeds, which, like her daughter, could emerge only in the spring and summer.

Our word for rice is derived from the ancient Greek *oriza*, which meant something like "originally from Asia," where in many places the general term for food is "rice." The Hindi word for rice, *dhanya*, translates roughly as "supporter of human beings." Rice has several origin myths. In South Asia, the goddess Kwan Yin is supposed to have dribbled her breast milk over barren grasses, which then yielded white rice. In Japan, legend has it that an undernourished priest discovered rice plants by following a mouse. And throughout Asia, rice is a mythic symbol of fertility, one prominently featured at traditional weddings. The widespread custom of throwing rice at newly married couples is thought to be derived from this ancient belief.

Then there is corn. Long known to the pre-Columbian peoples of the Americas, corn (maize) was not only the staple food of the Aztecs, Mayans, and other, more obscure groups, but also the basis on which many of their cultural practices and religious rituals were organized. There are many origin myths for corn, and most of them, like the Amazon Indian legend of a star coming to Earth in the form of a woman to teach men how to plant the cereal, involve a female protagonist. An Ecuadorean myth has it that a parrot turned into a woman, who then gave men corn seeds, whereas according to a rather sexist North American Indian story, corn first grew out of a furrow created when a mysterious woman instructed a man to drag her by the hair across an open field.

The presence of females as central enabling figures in so many food origin myths is no accident. Archaeological and anthropological research indicates that it was utterly clear to our prehistoric ancestors that women were not merely the bearers of new life but also the embodiment of nourishment and nurturance. Arbitrary as such myths may seem today, their emphasis on women as the progenitors of food persists in contemporary brand names such as Betty Crocker, Aunt Jemima, and Sara Lee. Indeed, the French still distinguish between "high" cuisine and everyday cooking by referring to them, respectively, as *cuisine gastronomique* and *cuisine de la femme* ("of the woman"). But the role of women, or female figures, in food myths is not always benign. One of the best-known mythic stories in Western civilization appears in the Old Testament: it is Eve who yields to the temptation of the forbidden apple and so gets all of us exiled from the Garden of Eden. And then there are the stories of witches with their poisonous apples and kettles full of nasty brews. For their part, male figures take on a central mythic role in connection with animal foods. According to the analyses of Central American tribal lore by Claude Lévi-Strauss in *The Raw and the Cooked*, it was the jaguar, which could take the form of a man, that first provided bows and arrows to male hunters, as well as the fire used to roast meat.

Mythic, magical ideas about food persist today in various forms. Fad health diets such as macrobiotics, which promises to prevent or cure cancer, are a good example. And underlying much of food advertising is the essentially magical notion that by consuming the foods endorsed by our modern secular gods—sports heroes are especially prominent here—we may identify more closely with them and perhaps participate in some of their achievements. Eating the "breakfast of champions" with the picture of a sports hero on its box may seem a far cry from swallowing the wafer and wine representing the body and blood of Christ in the Catholic Mass, but the underlying psychology is similar. Children are particularly susceptible to magical thinking, and I am sure I was not the only child of my generation who acquired a taste for raw carrots from watching Bugs Bunny cartoons. Carrots were also a central item in a modern bit of disinformation created by British propagandists during World War II. To help conceal the fact that their night fighter pilots were being guided to their targets by newly invented radar equipment, the British claimed they had improved their pilots' eyesight by having them eat raw carrots. This cover story was widely circulated, and, despite its fictitious origin, there may still be people today who believe that raw carrots can enhance night vision.

Clearly, marketing experts know very well that sports stars and other celebrities, no less than the gods of the ancients, embody and represent important social values, and that the foods they endorse or actually consume may symbolically represent these values. After spending much of his career studying the origins of food and cuisines, Claude Lévi-Strauss famously remarked about food preferences that what is "good to think is good to eat." Youngsters today eating their "breakfast of champions" may suspect that this will not make them a baseball or football star, but it is still "good to think." Knowingly or not, when eating, we are consuming not only the food item but also the concept that goes with it. Indeed, all the various cuisines — French, Chinese, Italian, and so forth — are arguably only sets of concepts that have made good after originally emerging in different regions of the world. Today, restaurants throughout the world offer variations of French, Chinese, or Italian cooking, and anyone having a Big Mac attack can find a McDonald's to satisfy it.

The burden of culturally significant meanings that particular foods carry was articulated in detail by French philosopher Roland Barthes. By way of example, he compared the North American preference for sweets — dairy bars, drinks, and the like — with the French preference for wine, suggesting that sugar and wine could be understood as cultural institutions because both are associated with a particular pattern of images, dreams, and values.

Another concept that is generally "good to think" is that the foods we eat are good for our health; this is often an important factor determining the meanings assigned to food. Is there any well-defined social group sharing a culture that does not believe its own cuisine is better tasting and healthier than any other? Religion has traditionally been the primary source of such beliefs. Long before the advent of advertising, news stories, and government information campaigns about the health hazards of indiscriminate eating habits, the health and metaphysical values associated with food were formally enshrined in the teachings of all major religions, as well as in the minor ones we typically call cults. Strict dietary regulations are observed by Orthodox Jews, Muslims, Hindus, Mormons, and, until the doctrinal changes of Vatican II, Catholics, who were forbidden to eat meat on Fridays. Protestant denominations are usually less stringent about food but, like other religions, encourage their followers to acknowledge eating as a sacred act by beginning each meal with a prayer of thanks. As well, in most if not all religions, certain food items are often reserved for special occasions and ceremonial use, as exemplified by the Jewish custom of eating unleavened bread *(matzoh)* on the Passover holiday, and by the Catholic use of wafers and wine.

Food consumption has been an object of significant religious attention and regulation for the same reasons as has sexual activity: both stand as central features determining the organization of human communities, and both can be powerful sources of the conflicts, anxieties, guilt feelings, and diseases that can destroy human communities. Both have always been, and still remain, fundamentally mysterious, because it is apparent that normal, responsible people every so often seem unable to avoid falling into serious problems over sex and food. The mystery here lies in the fact that both of these appetites have a way of periodically getting out of hand, slipping beyond the bonds of conscious control. We can become sexually aroused "against our will" in a dream or through random contact with a stranger or a suddenly attractive acquaintance, just as we can experience unexpected cravings for a double-fudge brownie or a hot dog smothered with sauerkraut. In short, our appetites can occasionally erupt without warning and push us—whether priests or presidents—right over the boundaries of rationality and morality. It makes perfect sense, then, that our premodern ancestors saw these experiences in terms of bewitchment or demonic possession. Phrases such as "The devil made me do it" and "I wasn't myself" suggest the presence of malevolent forces requiring a powerful religious defense. It seems likely that the practice of fasting on certain religious holidays began partly as an effort to discipline the appetites.

Rampant gluttony, however, has never been seen to be as much of a threat to orderly society as rampant sexuality has, and so has never received the same religious priority. Two of the Ten Commandments are warnings against illicit sex (adultery and coveting your neighbor's wife); none says anything about excessive eating or consuming forbidden foods. And while a great deal of publicity was given to the sexual behavior of celebrities such as Elvis Presley, Judy Garland, and Elizabeth Taylor, not to mention Bill Clinton, relatively little public attention focused on their eating habits and weight problems. Noteworthy in this context is that today in North America there are many over-the-counter drugs that suppress appetites for food but none that suppresses appetites for sex. Indeed, there is one expensive new item, Viagra, that can improve the capacity for sex, though so far only in males. At the time of writing this book, no major religions had issued any statements about Viagra, nor had they said much of anything about the relationships between food consumption and sexuality, a topic which has been left to the attention of psychoanalytic writers. In fact, we have much more systematic knowledge about the psychological meanings of sex than of food. Over the past hundred years, sex has been so thoroughly worked over from every conceivable perspective that as an area of study it has sunk into banality. By contrast, apart from the attention given to such still-unresolved problems as anorexia and bulimia, the common social and emotional dynamics associated with food have largely remained as a collection of unbreached mysteries.

One such mystery noted by Mary Douglas, who is considered by many to be the leading anthropological authority on food behavior, is why nutrition education fails. She has noted that, in modern societies, consumers seem just as conservative and resistant to the advice of nutrition experts as are rural peasants in underdeveloped areas of the world. George Orwell described such consumer irrationality concretely. Writing in the 1930s, he observed that welfare workers could not persuade the wives of unemployed Welsh miners to give up buying white bread in favor of more nutritious and less expensive black bread. Orwell called this a "peculiar evil" but went on to offer a psychological explanation based on his own experience of poverty that can also serve today as a good explanation for the popularity of fast foods among the urban poor. The thrust of it was that, when people are leading boring, unhappy lives, they are not interested in healthy foods but prefer anything that is stimulating, cheap, and convenient.

There are many other persistent mysteries about food preferences. Paul Rozin, who has been described quite justifiably as the "ultimate food psychologist," has suggested that no one really knows how food preferences are acquired. It is widely believed, for example, that we tend to grow up liking the foods that our parents like, yet Rozin's research shows that there is only a low correlation between the food preferences of parents and those of their children. He has also observed that there is no clear explanation for how it is that we can acquire tastes for foods that are initially off-putting, such as hot peppers.

The general feeling of bewilderment before human food behaviors that seems to occur among scholars and researchers who have spent their careers studying the subject was candidly summed up by another prominent authority, Sidney Mintz, who claimed to be "regularly astonished" by the eating habits of many Americans. The significance of such mysteries and astonishments—of which we have only scratched the surface—is that they demonstrate one of the fundamental principles underlying the focus of this book. It is precisely because so many of our common eating behaviors appear to be irrational that the social and psychological meanings of food are so powerful. In the absence of any standardized, objective system that can encompass and resolve the mysteries—a universally applicable "calculus" of food behaviors—the definition and meanings of food can be approached only by examining the relevant traditions, norms, and values that have evolved in particular cultures and social groups. These appear to be the strongest forces governing food consumption. As I noted in some of the examples described earlier, when people deviate by refusing to eat in accord with customary manners (try eating with your fingers in an expensive restaurant), or by eating something beyond the limits of what is locally accepted, they become the targets of powerful sanctions. Those who violate the food conventions of their group or society do so at their own risk.

But why do the mysteries underlying many of our eating behaviors remain unresolved despite the efforts of nutrition scientists, anthropologists, and other experts? Some of the reasons are fairly obvious, such as the fact that our food habits are so deeply embedded in taken-for-granted patterns of daily life that they are difficult to conceptualize as an object of study. As with air and water, so also with food: we think critically about it or see it as a problem worthy of serious attention only when faced with a shortage, contamination, or some other threat to its familiar status. In such circumstances, attention is primarily directed toward eliminating the threat with a quick fix rather than toward systematic study of the diverse ways foods are construed and take on their psychological meanings. And in addition to taking our own food habits for granted, we typically take for granted much of the ideological baggage carried by the food habits of others. The idea that every human group, from the family to the tribe to the modern nation-state, can be distinguished by its characteristic food habits, and even stigmatized accordingly as unworthy or disgusting, has never excited much theoretical attention except from a few anthropologists and students of slang about "krauts" or "limeys."

But a more important barrier to the scientific resolution of food mysteries is that food and eating habits refuse to stand still for analysis. It is often impossible to firmly define specific food preferences as being either the cause or the consequence of consumption behaviors. In other words, do we change our consumption attitudes because we have tried a particular food and enjoyed it, or do we try a particular food because we have changed our consumption attitudes? Depending on circumstances, it can be either one or both. Similarly, do we develop preferences for certain foods because we have had them frequently in the past and have gotten used to them as a source of pleasure? Or do we seek out certain foods because they have only seldom been available to us in the past and we look forward to them as a novel source of pleasure? There are no simple answers to these questions because, in principle, food can be construed as either cause or effect, or both.

Moreover, food does not stand still for analysis at the practical level. Freud could at least get his patients down on a couch, Skinner could keep his pigeons caged, and Pavlov had his dogs in special harnesses, but human food researchers have to deal with people who are in constant flux. People may respond differently to foods, or interviews about their eating habits, depending on the season of the year, the time of day, whether or not they happen to be hungry, whether they are getting over a cold or a broken love affair, and so forth. Appetites vary with emotions. In this context, groups appear more consistent than individuals because individual differences can be averaged, but here too the subject matter of preferences and eating habits is hard to pin down. In North America and many other parts of the world, children today not only do not eat what their parents ate when they were children but also eat food items that did not exist when their parents were children. According to one source of food marketing statistics, between 1950 and 1970 there was a threefold increase in the number of grocery items available to U.S. consumers, and this was before the advent of many newer convenience and microwave products. And quite apart from the steady stream of new items produced by the food industry, specific items from various regional cuisines seem to constantly emerge from their cultures of origin and become transformed into world-class items. You can now have, in one form or another, a pizza or burrito at any major airport in the world.

Finally, in addition to the endless changes occurring in *what* we eat, food researchers must contend with ongoing changes in *how* we eat. In the U.S. and other modern societies, the heavy, formal, home-cooked meals that once were considered a fundamental anchoring point of family life have become relics of the past, along with the laborious kitchen work and stylized table manners associated with such meals. Except on special occasions, family togetherness is now less likely to be rooted in the kitchen than in fast-food outlets or in front of the TV while eating microwaved slices of pizza. And even this togetherness may be disappearing, as family members are increasingly on different schedules, following different diets, or dealing with different food allergies.

Taken together, the growing diversity of what we eat and how we eat, as well as the difficulty of getting food to stand still for analysis, make it quite apparent that systematic research is not likely to resolve these food mysteries. Worse yet, given the seemingly unending, increasing variability of our food behaviors, any mystery that is finally resolved will probably be immediately replaced by several new ones. Is it any wonder, then, that under these conditions the majority of food research is carried out with laboratory rats? The difficulties facing food researchers further underscore the theme of this chapter: that the only viable approach to understanding the meanings of food is by recognizing and embracing the constant flow of changes in what we eat and how we eat.

When applying social theory to questions of the definition and meanings of food, however, we must first acknowledge that biological and psychological factors impose firm limits. No amount of purely social activity or discussion, for instance, can outweigh the fundamental facts of biology. It is clear that we cannot consume or be nourished by stones, and that humans everywhere show a preference for sweets and nowhere eat feces as a regular part of their diets. Nor is it difficult to appreciate the wide range of individual differences in our digestive systems, or the biochemical factors underlying certain food allergies.

By the same token, there is hardly any social activity pertaining to food that is not in some degree contingent on a broad range of psychological factors. Culturally conditioned personal values and attitudes, emotional traumas, various defense mechanisms, and developmental experiences may all play a role in how individuals and groups negotiate the meanings of food. Yet despite the many obvious limiting conditions imposed by biological and psychological factors, the main "agenda" establishing the definition and meanings of food is set by social factors. It is the larger social context over which we have little or no personal control that determines what range of foods will be available to us and what sorts of experiences will determine the values and attitudes associated with these foods. This begins during infancy and early childhood, in the relatively narrow framework of the family, and its scope progressively widens as people mature. As mentioned earlier, one all-too-familiar result is that, by the time they are teenagers and exposed to a broader variety of foods and food-related values and attitudes than are found in their families, many young people rebel against their parents' food habits. Just as every new generation produces its own styles of music, clothing, and slang expressions, it also contrives its own style of food and eating. Pizza "arrived" with the youth generation of the 1950s, granola with the '60s, salad bars and "grazing" with the '70s and '80s, and designer coffeehouses with the '90s.

Another useful way to understand the implications of social processes for the definition and meanings of food is through the philosophical concept of worldviews. Most philosophers and students of the human condition now accept that, as Ken Wilber, a prominent scholar of spiritual and religious practices, has summarized it, different ways of understanding the world around us have prevailed at different points in human history. Wilber argues that these have included (a) the primitive "magic-animistic" view, in which all objects in nature are seen as alive and endowed with souls or spirits; (b) the premodern "mythic" view, in which all natural phenomena, and the fates of humans as well, are controlled by gods or goddesses; and (c) the modern or "mental" view, characterized by rationality and the separation of nature into subjective and objective categories manageable by humans.

Although each has been dominant in different historical epochs, these views are all in one form or another still with us. Anthropologists know that many tribal groups maintain magic-animistic and mythic views, and developmental psychologists know that, in the Western world, young children progress from the magic-animistic to the mental-rational view by the time they reach adolescence. What is particularly relevant here about these views is the extent to which all three of them remain in force when it comes to the meanings of food. One might think they would have come and gone with historical changes in the major sources of food: magic-animistic views with foraging and hunting, mythic views with agriculture, and mental-rational views with industrial production of processed foods.

But these food views are directly or indirectly being acted out today throughout the underdeveloped, developed, and overdeveloped regions of the world. All are operative even in contemporary North America. Although direct forms of foraging via hunting and gathering (if only from the backyard garden) remain chiefly as a hobby for many people, we nevertheless have our symbolic types of foraging, as can be seen among those who search with a magic-animistic orientation through health-food stores, Internet pages, and obscure herbal texts. Other people show evidence of the mythic food view as they adopt dietary practices recommended by health gurus and medical celebrities. Meanwhile, most of us educated according to the mental-rational view scrutinize supermarket labels, attempting to follow the latest scientific calculus for optimum nutrition. This is not to say that everyone can be pigeonholed into one or another of these categories. Many of us act out all three categories at one time or another. How we do this in everyday life is considered in the following chapter, devoted to the normal range of differences between our food behaviors and what they may reveal or suggest about our personalities.

CHAPTER 2

You Are What You Eat

L IKE IT OR NOT, the way we eat is closely related to who we are or want to become. In effect, it is the personal and public presentation of self through food because, when it comes to personality, the uses of food are ubiquitous and often paradoxical, in the sense of being both inner and outer directed. That is, we may eat in ways aimed at the satisfaction of inner, personal needs, or in order to impress others. Our food behavior can therefore be personal and covert (some people eat only as they truly wish to when no one is looking) or, like our clothing, part of our contrived public image. In the latter category is a perennial item of folk wisdom widely circulated among young women in North America: never order spaghetti on a dinner date. I first heard this from my older sister more than fifty years ago, and since then it has been confirmed many times over by young women in my college classes who know that it's hard to look attractive while eating spaghetti. However, there is no consensus on which foods can make women seem more attractive. My wife claims that the best rule is no drippy items, and only small bites of everything else.

Another variation on this theme involves casual and calculated efforts to explore the character of others by observing their

eating behaviors. Hence the invitation to dine with your potential boss when being considered for a responsible position, or
the invitation to dinner from concerned parents who think you
might be seriously interested in their marriageable daughter or
son. Then, too, there is the use of food in fiction. Novelists
and filmmakers frequently amplify the characters they create
by dramatizing their food habits. James Bond is portrayed as a
gourmet, ordering his martinis shaken, not stirred, whereas
Dirty Harry has a hot dog for lunch. In the film *Pulp Fiction*,
two of the main characters are hired killers who are "human-
ized" for the audience when they discuss the quality of hamburgers sold by McDonald's in Amsterdam. And feminist
writers have noted that "good women" in films such as *Babette's
Feast* and *Like Water for Chocolate* are defined by the pains-
taking preparation of foods they serve to others but hardly eat
themselves. "Bad women," on the other hand, tend to be shown
as careless consumers.

The point is that one of the most common and relatively
subtle but important ways we get to know others, gaining
impressions of their personalities, is through their eating habits.
Social psychology studies have demonstrated that people will
make fairly consistent judgments of others based on their
grocery shopping lists. Equally important is that people come
to judge *themselves* through their eating habits. Consider the
insult added to injury when people with weight problems yield
to the temptation of an extra helping of pizza or a high-calorie
dessert and then indict themselves, feeling depressed about their
lack of willpower. Paradoxically, people can become depressed
when they violate their diets, but they are most likely to violate
their diets when they feel depressed. There are also those people

who keep their special, usually fattening, goodies hidden away for private binges—binges after which they feel guilty. But paradoxically again, such guilt can have its bright side when friends or lovers discover the delicious intimacy of shared guilt from bingeing together on "forbidden" foods. My own experience of the link between eating behavior and self-esteem has been along a very different tangent. I found that, as a young soldier, I could more or less enjoy eating almost anything at any time and under any conditions. On field exercises in freezing weather, for example, when the hash in our mess tins was congealing together with the fruit cocktail and mashed potatoes, I could scoff it all up quite greedily, while many around me were dumping it in the mud. The result was that, although some might take this as evidence of piggishness, I gained a spurious sense of superiority based on the premise of owning a cast-iron stomach.

Along with table manners, food preferences can play a substantial role in how people judge the social class status of themselves and others. It has been noted by culture critics such as Roland Barthes and Paul Fussell that poorly educated, low-income people generally prefer sweet foods. This theme was elaborated by Fussell, who suggested that one can identify a person's social class by his or her drinking habits. According to Fussell, if you like sweet drinks—rum and Coke, whiskey and 7-up—you are definitely "prole," particularly if you serve these drinks in juice glasses decorated with cute animal pictures. He further stipulates that the upper-class drinks are white wine, vodka, and scotch and water, and, if drinking before three in the afternoon, Bloody Marys.

There are at least three plausible psychological explanations of why strong preferences for sweet foods and drinks are associated with low social status. First, sweets are the most immediate gratification treats for children. Adults with a sweet tooth may appear childish, whereas restraining their desire for sweets may point to mature self-discipline, the ability to control vulgar appetite. Moreover, if the masses are like children in their food preferences, it behooves the elite to demonstrate their superiority by rejecting those preferences. There is also the Marxist interpretation suggesting that cheap sweets serve as a type of pacifier for workers condemned to a life of alienated labor. The harsher the conditions of one's life, the more one may crave any sort of immediate visceral pleasure.

Food is also often seen as an indicator of gender identity. Systematic marketing studies conducted in the 1950s and '60s by the psychoanalyst Ernst Dichter showed that meats, potatoes, and coffee were considered strongly masculine by consumers, whereas rice, cake, and tea were seen as feminine. These and other, more recent, studies have shown a relatively clear pattern of traditional sexism associated with many foods. Most "light" foods—salads, yogurt, fruit—have a feminine image, while heavy, smelly foods—herring, pot roast, corned beef, and cabbage—are seen as masculine. The linkage between these food stereotypes and those relating to typical male and female body images hardly requires elaboration. Some foods, however, such as chicken and oranges, were found by Dichter to be "bisexual," or gender neutral.

The imagery associated with a food can carry emotional significance for many people. Eating masculine or feminine foods, for example, can be important for teenagers struggling with gender identity. And there were probably many children like me who acquired an appetite for spinach from watching Popeye cartoons, which showed the green as a source of strength and power. There is also probably a fair number of adults who were first moved to try drinking a dry martini after seeing one of the James Bond films. Dichter concluded that people develop preferences for foods that represent the type of person they admire or identify with. And conversely, people may develop aversions to foods that are associated with characters they dislike. Dichter's findings are clearly relevant to the discussion of magical thinking introduced in the previous chapter.

Anthropological research indicates that the process at work here is fundamentally primitive. It can be traced back to our hunter ancestors, who apparently admired powerful animals and believed that they could gain some of that strength by eating parts of the animals' bodies—the heart of a lion, perhaps, or even something from the dead body of a powerful enemy warrior. A contemporary variation on this theme harks back to the social class implications of food. People trying to move into a higher social class are likely to modify their food habits—abandoning McDonald's and Pizza Hut in favor of more up-scale restaurants. They may also start buying their groceries at specialty shops instead of at supermarkets. (It is noteworthy that many supermarkets now have expensive gourmet-food departments.)

But food behaviors are not only a means by which people attempt to improve their social position or take on admired qualities of a celebrity. They are also, often more profoundly, a reflection of deep-seated personality qualities that are resistant to change. Although one might shift from hamburgers to filets mignons, from sardines to caviar, and from instant coffee to rare blends, the way the food is approached and consumed may remain the same. It's not necessary to study psychoanalytic theory to recognize the obsessive-compulsive tendencies shown by people who insist on arranging the food on their plates in a certain pattern; having their bread toasted lightly, darkly, or in-between; or having their coffee not too hot and not too cold and with just the right amount of sugar and cream. All forms of obsessive behavior—and it is no mere coincidence that, in addition to food habits, it often shows up in toilet behaviors—can be understood as defenses against anxiety. People who show obsessive food behaviors are evidently attempting to cope with anxieties that probably can be traced to harsh or traumatic childhood experiences with eating.

At the other extreme are those who seem indifferent to their food: indiscriminate hearty eaters like the men—and they are most often men, not women—described by friends or family as garbage disposals because they clean everyone else's plate as well as their own. Having acted similarly myself as a soldier, I may be somewhat biased about the psychological sources of such behavior, but two plausible interpretations can be made. The benign view is that such robust food behavior reflects a relatively unconflicted, confident personality, based on a pattern of satisfying, pleasurable food experiences during childhood. In short, the happy, hearty eater may be just that—someone who enjoys food. Recall the famous remark of Sigmund Freud, who, when asked about the psychological significance of his cigar smoking (an oral fixation?), is supposed to have replied "Sometimes a cigar is just a cigar."

A less benign view of garbage disposal eating is that people unable to express their anxieties about food—because those anxieties are so threatening to their self-esteem—attempt to cope by denying them. In this view, the excessively fast, indiscriminate eater is like the male who adopts a hypermacho style as a way of dealing with his anxieties about homoerotic feelings. Heavy, rapid eating may be a habitual adult defense against the childhood fear of not getting enough or of food not being available the next time he or she is hungry.

Another, quite different, social psychological use of food can be seen in people who exploit it as a form of sublimation. A good example of this is self-styled gourmets who cultivate an elaborate sensual-aesthetic interest in eating and take every opportunity to show this off in public by cross-examining waiters, discoursing on recipes, or criticizing the uneducated tastes of the masses. On Monday mornings, these people will often talk about a great meal they had over the weekend the way others talk about a great film or football game they saw. Because such gourmet pretensions are increasingly accepted in our society as evidence of sophisticated cultural values, they provide convenient compensation for people who have failed to realize their cultural aspirations more directly through intellectual or artistic accomplishments. And preoccupation with cooking gourmet meals for oneself or others may be the expression of unfulfilled sexual desires. The psychoanalytic view of sublimation suggests that stimulation or manipulation of another person's taste sensations can be a sensual experience analogous to seduction, whereas preparing elaborate special dishes to be eaten alone implies sensual self-gratification.

None of these patterns of consumption need be considered seriously pathological unless it is carried to an extreme, yet each can speak volumes about individual personality dynamics—namely, the various ways individuals have learned to use food consumption as a means of managing and expressing their emotions. But given the inevitable disappointments we all occasionally experience in everyday life, it is probably fortunate that occasional brief periods of self-indulgent eating allow us to realize the all-purpose remedy reflected in the saying "Living well is the best revenge." This principle is acted on by many people who have learned to deal with emotional depressions by treating themselves to comfort foods. In her novel *Heartburn*, Nora Ephron's protagonist recuperates from failed love affairs by taking to her bed to eat large bowls of creamy mashed potatoes. According to students in my classes, other popular comfort foods include chicken soup, and cocoa and cookies, items they were given as children to eat during an illness or while recovering from an injury. A perfect example of the comfort phenomenon appeared in a 1994 news story during Bill Clinton's first term as U.S. president. Apparently, one evening the Clintons' daughter, Chelsea, was not feeling well. Her mother wanted to make Chelsea her favorite scrambled eggs; the White House staff wanted to prepare an omelette. Hillary Clinton had to insist that only she knew how to make the appropriate comfort food for her daughter.

As parents, one of the first things we learn is that, apart from the emotional attachments children may develop to certain foods, their general emotional state is often directly evident from the way they eat. Any serious emotional or physical problem is nearly always signaled by an apparent loss of appetite. Of course, common experience suggests that this is also true for many adults. Studies have shown that, for many normal adults, food consumption is lowest when they are experiencing serious pain, stress, or anger. (This is discussed in more detail later in the chapter.) It is much easier, however, to see this effect of emotional distress in children. The comfort-food phenomenon ties in directly here because it generally grows out of parental efforts to encourage children to eat by offering them something they particularly enjoy. Also interesting is that the more comforting items are usually starches rather than sweets such as ice cream or candy. Parents may not know this except through trial and error, but, according to dietary experts, it is based on a physiological fact: starchy carbohydrates such as potatoes, macaroni, and rice are metabolized much more slowly than sugars and have a calming effect on the emotions—just what we want for kids when they are upset. Sweets, on the other hand, are quickly assimilated in the body and elevate the emotions.

It should be apparent now why it is that what we eat, how we eat it, and the idiosyncratic ways in which these behaviors may serve our social and emotional needs can all be seen as manifestations of our personal style of being in the world. In short, our anxieties, aspirations, and modes of relating to others are embodied in our food habits. These habits are as unique as our fingerprints and much more revealing of who we are. But how did we get this way? How do our food habits emerge, develop, and become a firmly embedded quality of our personality? Fortunately, there is substantial research bearing on this topic.

According to some of the newest findings, our taste preferences start developing well before birth. Research has shown that the fetus begins to occasionally swallow amniotic fluid at about the twelfth week of its development. When sweet and bitter solutions are injected into the amniotic fluid, there is more swallowing of the sweet fluid. Another study has shown that premature babies prefer a sweet solution to plain water. Depending on her diet, the mother's amniotic fluid may have a distinctive odor. Researchers report that, when pregnant women swallowed garlic capsules, their amniotic fluid later smelled of garlic. These studies, as well as related work done with prenatal and postnatal animals, strongly suggest that food preferences emerge before and immediately after birth. Young sheep, pigs, and rodents have been found to prefer, after weaning, flavors they experienced earlier in their mother's milk.

Additional evidence that taste preferences develop early on has come from research with mothers nursing healthy infants. Two hours after nursing mothers swallowed either garlic or vanilla capsules, these flavors showed up strongly in their breast milk. In both cases, the infants responded favorably by sucking more of the flavored milk, as compared with prior sucking of the unflavored milk. It appears that an infant's appetite, like that of most adults, is stimulated by novel flavors, although, as with adults, the novelty wears off after repeated experience with the new flavors, and infants return to their usual sucking pattern. (An interesting offshoot of these studies is that a number of hospitals in North America, and parts of Europe as well, now provide new mothers with vanilla-flavored pacifiers for their babies.) Infants do not, however, respond favorably to all novel flavors; alcohol in breast milk resulted in less sucking. It has also been suggested that infants fed with only standard baby formulas are deprived of many early sensory experiences with food. This causes them to miss out on experiences that would prepare them for the diverse flavors available in their environment, making them likely to be more resistant to novel foods later on.

A wide range of genetic factors can also influence food preferences. Just as we inherit our body characteristics, such as eye color, hair color, and body type, we also inherit particular digestive systems. The range of differences between normal individuals can be quite large. For example, postmortem studies indicate that stomach-lining tissue may vary in its thickness by a factor of over 100 percent in normal populations. If it is true that a thick stomach lining tends to protect against gastric distress, the thickness of a child's stomach lining is probably one of the factors explaining a child's eating habits—habits which lead to that child being labeled as a good, picky, or poor eater.

Some of the latest research on physiological differences between individuals also concerns taste sensitivities. There are apparently large differences between individuals in our inherited taste traits, based on the number of taste receptors in our tongues. Those of us with more receptors—usually women—have been categorized by researchers as "supertasters" and are estimated to make up about 25 percent of the North American population, whereas another 25 percent with substantially fewer receptors are considered "nontasters." Supertasters are particularly sensitive to the flavors of ginger, alcohol, and chili peppers and tend to reject bitter-tasting items such as coffee, spinach, brussels sprouts, and cabbage. These findings go a long way toward explaining the biological basis of individual food preferences and suggest that there may be more than simple sexism underlying cultural stereotypes about masculine and feminine foods.

It is clear that, beyond the genetic, prenatal, and neonatal considerations that provide the foundation for many of our basic food behaviors, subsequent food experiences—from early childhood to the end of adolescence—can profoundly modify our early predispositions. This is one area where the common experiences most of us have growing up and the conclusions reached by leading authorities on individual food preferences are in near-perfect agreement. The preferences and aversions we acquire throughout our formative years of development are the products of associations that occur between particular foods and particular social, psychological, and biological states. In fact, it's fair to say that the closest thing we have to a general principle underlying food preferences that is applicable across the board—from individuals to families, groups, and whole societies—is the "law of association." In practice, this means that all of us learn, through simple conditioning mechanisms, to associate certain foods with positive or negative feelings.

During infancy, for example, even the act of nursing at the mother's breast is susceptible to conditioning. Like Pavlov's dogs, which learned to associate feeding with the sound of a bell, human infants quickly learn to anticipate feeding (indicated by their reflexive sucking response) from the sights and sounds of their mothers preparing to nurse. In one controlled experiment, each mother wore a red bib each time she nursed. After a number of repetitions, the infants would begin reflexive sucking when shown the red bib—a fine example of classical conditioning. Associations between the satisfaction of hunger and the mother's presence are apparently pleasurable if the mother is a consistently good provider and the circumstances are relaxed. But if she is not, and if the feeding experience is often disturbed or upsetting, such associations may induce anxiety. In extreme cases, the association with anxiety can continue into adulthood, becoming the basis for either habitual tense behavior in food situations or obsessive eating rituals that serve as a defense against the anxiety.

During childhood, food aversions are quite common and can arise from a variety of experiences that can create intense negative associations with specific items. For instance, children often have a spontaneously aversive reaction to the sight, smell, and taste of oatmeal and other hot mushy cereals. Well-meaning parents frequently make matters worse by attempting to cajole or force their child to eat the cereal because "it's good for you." In some of my own research where college students were asked to give free associations to various common foods, many of their responses to oatmeal were viscerally negative: "Ugh!" "Library paste!" "Forced to eat it as a child!" But a few were positive, recalling cold winter mornings and the pleasure of hot oatmeal smothered with brown sugar. Presumably, enough sugar makes anything go down. Threats and cajolery, however, won't work. When parents employ contingency strategies—the promise of rewards or punishments—to get their children to try new foods, they usually fail. And if such efforts are accompanied by a high level of tension so that the food becomes a focus of parent–child conflict, the result can simply be to strengthen the child's aversion.

A dramatic illustration of how specific food aversions can result from a single, traumatically conditioned association is described in the book *Our Own Worst Enemy* by the British psychologist Norman Dixon. The incident occurred while Dixon was a child at a boarding school, where the daily breakfast was lumpy porridge. One morning, the boy next to him was having a hard time breaking apart a large lump in his bowl. He finally succeeded, and, to Dixon's horror, the lump contained a dead mouse. Since then, Dixon has never been able to eat porridge. Less dramatic but similarly powerful are the often-accidental experiences that can produce an aversion. An item may be too hot to swallow and burn the tongue; it may be too highly spiced; the child may be ill and throw up; or there may be an intense family quarrel at the table. All these situations can create negative associations with food items that may persist into adulthood and even through one's entire life.

Positive associations, such as those with comfort foods, are also quite frequent. One of the typical variations on this theme, which can be either positive or negative, is the association we often make between people and their distinctive eating habits. To this day, whenever I encounter Gruyère, I am reminded of a college girlfriend who always brought a little package of *vache qui rit* Gruyère to nibble on when we went to the movies. In addition to the associations unique to individuals, we all share many culturally defined associations between foods and special occasions or holidays, such as turkey and Thanksgiving. This is because they are so prevalent. In one of my studies with college students, popular free associations to hot dogs were family picnics and baseball games. And among former soldiers of my generation, Spam and creamed chipped beef (the famous SOS: "shit on a shingle") invariably evoke the military.

Different types of music are also consistently linked with different cuisines, apparently on the basis of shared cultural stereotypes. Some of my research shows that most undergraduates associated country and western with barbecue and fried chicken; rock and roll with pizza and hamburgers; and classical music with lobster and filet mignon. Such simple food associations can occur and persist at any age. But as we move into adolescence and adulthood, they are likely to become more complex and much more a result of higher cognitive processes, processes that can override those associations that have been reflexively conditioned. In effect, through acts of will—by deliberately conditioning themselves—people may drastically alter their food preferences. This occurs frequently: many people decide as a matter of moral conviction or personal health to follow a vegetarian diet and then find that after a while they no longer have any desire for meat.

Less dramatic but no less significant are many of the other ways in which conceptual thinking begins to alter teenagers' preexisting food preferences. The proverbial peer pressure may influence not only their hair and clothing styles but also their eating habits. This conformity to group norms can be especially conspicuous among first- or second-generation American teenagers, who tend to reject the traditional ethnic foods of their families in favor of popular "American" cuisine. An example of this involving Mexican-American adolescents in the 1930s and '40s is described in Harvey Levenstein's 1993 history of changing American food habits. Ashamed of the tacos packed for their school lunches, these teenagers would throw them away or try to trade them for peanut butter and jelly sandwiches. Ironically, fifty years later, "Americanized" tacos and burritos became favorite items among almost all teenagers.

Developmental research suggests that, in addition to peer-group conformity, changes in teenagers' food habits stem from a drive to explore novel experiences, which may include everything from drinking beer to smoking cigarettes to putting ketchup on pizza. And when exposure to American films, TV shows, music videos, and advertising is ciphered into the mix, it is no wonder that, throughout Europe, Asia, and Latin America, teenagers are usually the best customers when a McDonald's or Pizza Hut arrives in town. A further impetus for change may simply come from new information. Adolescents in athletic programs may begin to follow the dietary recommendations of their coaches, while other teenagers exposed to nutrition science or material extolling the virtues of vegetarianism may also be motivated to change their diet.

Among teenagers, girls typically go through the most dramatic dietary changes because of concerns about their appearance. Innumerable studies have shown weight-reduction dieting of one sort or another to be virtually epidemic among young women and girls, and for many it begins as early as pre-adolescence. In the more extreme instances, which are by no means uncommon, food bingeing and purging (bulimia), self-starvation (anorexia), and heavy use of appetite-suppressing drugs such as amphetamines can create serious health problems. This issue of dieting, and how it can shade into one or another serious eating disorder, will be discussed in detail in chapter 3 but deserves emphasis here too because it demonstrates the power of cognitive factors—images and ideals about physical attractiveness—to override established eating habits and hunger.

When viewed across the entire life span, food habits stand out as most likely to be changeable, unstable, and potentially a threat to health during both adolescence and old age. The reasons for this are quite obvious and in some ways very similar. These are the two periods in life when the most radical changes occur in both our physiology and our social environments. Our food habits are pushed toward change from both the inside (biology) and the outside (society). Although the impacts of these changes are typically more intense and take place in a shorter time frame during adolescence, gradual changes among the elderly can also be profound. With advanced age there is a decline in taste sensitivity, which at least partially explains why so many older people complain that the bread (or other foods) these days just doesn't taste as good as it did when they were young. Chewing can also become more difficult because of dental or jaw muscle problems, and so dietary preferences shift toward softer items. Changes among the elderly also can occur quite suddenly. Older adults are notoriously subject to injuries or other acute health problems that may radically alter their lifestyles and eating behaviors. A seventy or eighty year old who falls and breaks an ankle or hip may become depressed and lose his or her appetite; an older person taking certain medications may feel nauseated.

Another similarity between adolescents and the elderly is their susceptibility to unhealthy food habits brought on by social factors: peer pressure among teenagers, and the loss of social support and stimulation often experienced by the elderly. The effects these conditions have on the food habits of the two groups can vary a great deal, but they generally push teenagers toward eating junk foods, impulse-driven "grazing," and fad dieting. The effect of social isolation on older adults is depression, loss of interest in eating, and a relatively impoverished diet, which in extreme cases can amount to slow starvation. This last effect is most likely to occur among those elderly who may also suffer from chronic illnesses or physical impairments limiting their ability to shop for groceries and prepare meals. (Food and aging are discussed further in chapter 4.)

During the long march through the middle years that separate the end of adolescence from old age, food habits generally remain stable except for variations associated with new convenience items and new technologies, such as microwave cooking. Two exceptions to this generalization concern gender and life crises. The gender "effect" reported in many studies, including one of mine in 1993, is simply that women are typically much more aware of the health aspects of food than men are. This distinction begins to show up in survey data from young, newly married women, who frequently say they feel responsible for the health of their husbands and try to encourage them to adopt healthier diets. This is particularly prominent among women who become pregnant and have their first child. Nutrition knowledge and concern remain higher for women than men all the way through old age. In surveys of retired people, we consistently found that women generally knew more about the nutritional values of foods and attached greater importance to this when describing their eating habits.

Life crises of one sort or another also affect food habits. Profound changes in diet almost always accompany any event that seriously alters a person's lifestyle. Marriage, divorce, the birth of a child, major financial loss or gain, illness, or injury — in short, any event that can be seen as a crisis or turning point in one's life, and some that are less intense — will, for better or worse, have its effect on eating behavior. The settling-down influence of marriage and child rearing usually leads to greater concern with healthy food choices, as does any experience with serious illness. But appetites and preferences can vary immensely and change rapidly among people dealing with life crises. Some may respond by eating less, paying close attention to weight-loss diets, and adopting ascetic cuisines or vegetarianism. Others eat more, try elaborate new recipes, and fall back into the impulsive habits of their adolescence. These alternatives are not mutually exclusive; I have known people in crisis situations who shifted from one to the other and back again within the space of a week. Few things influence adult food behaviors as much as a major life crisis, and it is no exaggeration to suggest that, in many cases, people respond with a manic-depressive pattern of eating, up one day and down the next.

Eating is also a conspicuous indicator of temporary emotional states, particularly all the variations from sadness to happiness. For some people, eating is like smoking or drinking; they do more of it at either emotional extreme, using food to celebrate when happy and to comfort themselves when depressed. But for most of us, appetite varies up or down depending on our position on the happy–sad scale. And then there are those occasional states we call "moody," when we may feel hungry for something without knowing just what that something is. Freudian theory would interpret this as a sign of free-floating anxiety, probably related to some sort of repressed hostility or desire concerning relationships associated with food. The repressed emotion is experienced as wanting something that cannot be consciously acknowledged. Projecting the emotion onto food provides a relatively acceptable way for it to be expressed.

One further dimension of food habits demanding attention here concerns the morality of food—the moral values associated with eating behaviors. Gluttony, for instance, is considered a venial sin among Catholics; obedience to the laws defining kosher foods is an imperative for Orthodox Jews; Muslims are forbidden pork; and in all religions it is considered immoral to waste food. We begin to acquire a sense of the morality of food virtually at our mother's breast, because this is where our eating behavior starts to generate good-bad moral judgments. Without any deliberation or conscious thought, virtually every mother will perceive the robust, uncomplaining eater to be the good infant or child, and the fussy, picky eater to be the bad, or at least not so good, child. These maternal reactions are conveyed to children in innumerable ways, so that already in early childhood a sense of moral worth is attached to eating. This might be represented by the commonsense reasoning that "to eat good is to make mother happy, to make mother happy is to *be* good." And, lest there be any doubt, a mother's pride in her good eater is invariably confirmed by the praise and approval she and her child receive from others. But, in contemporary North America, where obesity is often viewed as a kind of secular sin, such praise can evaporate, replaced by disapproval if by the age of five or six the child has become conspicuously overweight.

A strong theoretical case can be made for the claim that eating behavior stands as a major foundation for the development of the Freudian superego, or moral conscience. But we need not accept Freud's theory of morality in order to recognize that ideas about right and wrong, good and bad, begin to take shape very early in life. Indeed, most authorities on child development agree that newborns are sensitive to, and tend to internalize, the positive or negative feelings of their mothers when nursing. And as babies mature, these internalized feelings become the rudimentary basis for their emerging sense of self. What begins to be established here is the emotional distinction between what psychiatrist Harry Stack Sullivan called the "good me" and the "bad me." General notions of good and bad, and right and wrong, quickly and unmistakably emerge when young children begin to be present at the family table, when they are praised or scolded depending on their consumption — how much they eat — and their manners — how much of a mess they make.

Any parent will know that teaching young children to handle a spoon or a cup and refrain from playfully or angrily throwing food is no small thing. And most parents also discover, sometimes to their chagrin, that they themselves will frequently be judged by others based on their child's table manners. It is a truism that the ways people conduct themselves at the table — including the whole range of behaviors comprising the etiquette of eating in every human society — frequently serve as a basis for moral value judgments: to eat like a pig is to be unworthy of respect and is seen as ignorant, greedy, or immoral. Judgments of social class status follow suit: the worse the manners, the lower the social class.

In his masterwork on the history of table manners first published in 1939, sociologist Norbert Elias traces the rise of Western civilization by tracking the evolution of manners from the Middle Ages to the modern era. He describes the increasing complexity of table manners across time and how they trickled down from the aristocracy to the masses. Elias further emphasizes that, through the centuries, the civilizing process can be seen as increasingly suppressing instinctive responses (grabbing, gobbling, spitting, slurping) in favor of artificially acquired skills and restraints. There is an obvious parallel here between the history of manners, including its moral implications, and the life experiences of children, who typically start out in their highchairs grabbing, gobbling, and spitting.

The moral dimension of food also embraces cuisine—the items deemed suitable to eat and the manner in which they are prepared. We learn quite early in childhood that, in addition to right and wrong ways of eating, there are also right and wrong cuisines. "Ours" is right and superior and smells good; "theirs" is wrong and inferior and smells bad, no matter whom "they" are. Our cuisine is whatever we have become familiar with in our family and ethnic in-group (the group to which we belong); their cuisine is whatever the out-group consumes. Ethnocentric food preferences are easily converted into food prejudices. These may then be used as moralistic justifications for social stereotyping and egocentric pretensions to superiority, the commonsense reasoning being that only inferior people would consume inferior foods. This explains why food has traditionally been a prominent feature of ethnic slurs. Probably because of North America's multiethnic population, American English provides a rich vocabulary of examples; we have "krauts" for Germans, "beaners" for Mexicans, "mackerel snappers" for Catholics, to name just a few.

Food also plays a prominent role in ethnic humor aimed at ridiculing various groups. The 1990 encyclopedic study of ethnic humor around the world by anthropologist Christie Davies contains an entire chapter devoted to insult jokes based on food and cuisine stereotypes. Some of these are quite mild, such as the one about the Norwegian and the Dane:

Norwegian: "Did you ever eat *ludefisk*?"

Dane: "No, but I think I stepped in some once."

Another is a French put-down of the British. After listening to a Frenchman talk about the superiority of French cuisine, the Englishman responds by saying, "Yes, but what about your dreadful lavatories?" To which the Frenchman replies, "*Alors*, in France one eats well, in England one shits well, it's all a question of priorities."

The idea that the food consumed by the out-group is garbage comes up frequently in various forms: "How do you know that a Texas Aggie is a galloping gourmet? You'll see him running after a garbage truck." Or this easily reversible item: "How do they dispose of garbage in Italian (or Polish) restaurants? They put it on the menu in Polish (or Italian) restaurants." Then there are the uglier ones, such as "Why do the Mexicans eat refried beans? Because they can never get things right the first time." And "How do you solve the Puerto Rican (or Mexican, or Asian) immigration problem? Convince the blacks that they taste like fried chicken." All these jokes are bad, and I've not mentioned many others that are even worse—less humorous and more offensive. But I do have a personal favorite. It's a *New Yorker* cartoon showing a frog seated at a table in an upscale restaurant, with a napkin tucked in its shirt. The frog expostulates: "Waiter! There's no fly in my soup!"

Apart from the bad jokes, ethnocentric attitudes about food extend beyond simple stereotypes to the acceptance or rejection of specific items in different cultures and religions. Beef rates high in America and low in India; puppy dogs are a treat in parts of Asia, as are raw-fish dishes and whale meat in Japan. Most Americans reject kidneys, frog legs, and snails; Orthodox Jews and Muslims reject pork. Regional and subcultural distinctions exist as well. Prairie oysters (bulls' testicles) and rattlesnake meat are acceptable in parts of the western U.S. but not elsewhere. All these preferences, whether pro or con, carry either implicit or explicit moral implications based on the principle "You are what you eat." Cultural norms and religious traditions are such that our food habits are an important element of the moral values intrinsic to our self-concepts, as well as to how we judge others. Nor is there much rationality or objectivity in all this; the moral implications are experienced as a gut reaction. You might be able to love someone who once swallowed a live goldfish, but it would be much more difficult to care for someone who dines regularly on roast puppy dogs or fried worms.

There is no convenient way to summarize the various direct and indirect connections between food and personality discussed in this chapter because they exist at so many different levels of human experience. The moment we look beyond its biological functions, eating can be seen as relevant to nearly every aspect of personality. As an expressive behavior, how we eat (fast or slow, our manners), what we eat (our preferences), and how much we eat (our quantities) can be linked directly to many personality traits. Tendencies toward conformity, creativity, rigidity, aggressiveness, self-confidence, and anxiety are all in one way or another likely to reveal themselves at the table. In this sense, one can "read" a person's habitual food behaviors for cues to his or her personality the way one reads the results of a projective personality test.

It is at this point that the general range of normal, commonly experienced connections between food and personality begins to shade into the domain of uncommon connections, namely psychopathology. And it is precisely this, the psychopathology of food, which is taken up in the following chapter.

CHAPTER 3

Feeding Frenzies

FUNDAMENTALLY, there are just two major food pathologies in our society: eating too much and eating too little. The former is more prevalent, but both have steadily increased over the past few decades, and both are important because, when pushed to their extremes, they are killers. Extreme obesity is associated with various health problems, the most deadly of which begins with hypertension and can end in death from heart disease. At the other extreme, self-starvation begins with dieting, can progress to bulimia and anorexia, and can end in death from malnutrition. This is not to say that there are no other pathologies or near pathologies centered on food; these will be considered soon enough. Meanwhile, it should be kept in mind that the pathologies, or eating disorders, are important not only because they are a problem for many people but also because they reveal the complex social and psychological dynamics that can distort food behaviors.

In general, when someone's eating habits cross the line from mild eccentricity to seriously weird or bizarre, they are almost always symptomatic of borderline or more serious neurotic anxieties. But while compulsive behaviors such as eating only one item at a time from the plate, or intensively scrutinizing and wiping silverware lest it be contaminated—two of the more common obsessive habits symptomatic of neurotic anxiety—may indicate a need for therapy, they are not in the same life-threatening league as excessive obesity and self-starvation. And although the self-abuse of people categorized as anorexic or bulimic appears far more mysterious to most of us than extreme obesity, which is usually attributed to simple gluttony, obesity is actually equally or more mysterious because it involves a complex mix of genetic, cultural, physiological, and emotional factors.

The most general approach to the mysteries of obesity has been formulated by the nutrition and dietary expert David Booth in the question "Why do we now not like being fat?" The question should not be dismissed as mere rhetoric. It points to a recent and profoundly significant change in the social and emotional meanings of food and our ideas about our bodies. Up through the end of the 19th century and the early years of the 20th century, we *did* like being fat. Fat had obvious survival value as protection against the effects of starvation in a world where local food shortages and widespread famines were not unusual. And it still does in parts of Africa, Asia, and the former Soviet Union. In almost all human societies, being fat was also a conspicuous sign of material success and high social status for both men and women. Yet today in North America and most of Europe, fat means just the opposite. It is the poor who are most likely to be fat, and the rich and famous, particularly women, who embody the aphorism "You can never be too rich or too thin." How did this reversal happen? Why is possessing a well-padded body or indulging in the joy of eating to the limit no longer desirable in modern societies?

The politically correct response today would simply be "health." But the widespread prejudice, in many cases revulsion, against obesity in our society today is not mainly due to the medical risks that have become common knowledge over the past thirty years. It is much more a matter of aesthetics and, perhaps even more importantly, a psychological effect of the new industrial and urban environments that emerged most emphatically in North America and Western Europe early in the 20th century. Most discussions of this topic only note that changes in aesthetic values and fashion styles are responsible for the trend away from the bulky, heavier bodies admired during the 19th century and earlier. They give little attention to the question of why this trend occurred. But closer scrutiny suggests that the answer involves a combination of biological, social, and psychological adaptations to industrial modernity. With the advent of the machine age and all the technological changes associated with it, including new food processing, distribution, and consumption patterns, heavy bodies became as obsolete as the horse-and-buggy, labor-intensive activities that once justified them.

A well-fleshed, bulky body with substantial fat reserves is clearly very desirable if you are working outdoors in all sorts of weather or shoveling coal for a living. But if you are in a protected indoor environment working at tasks that require little muscular effort, such a heavy body is essentially useless. And from the standpoint of prevalent social class values, it is also stigmatizing, in the same way that rough work boots and bib overalls stigmatize or define a person as low-end working class. On the other hand, to have a thin, unupholstered body is to be marked as fragile: unfit for the heavy outdoor work or frequent childbearing reserved for "the masses," but well adapted to office work and driving cars with automatic transmissions. In short, and as Marxist theorists might put it, with the rise of industrial modernity, the body begins to lose its "use value" while gaining "exchange value." It takes on a symbolic meaning indicative of social class status and becomes valued less for its survival uses against heavy work or harsh weather than for its decorative or aesthetic functions. In fact, according to current health statistics, it is now just the opposite, because in modern societies thin bodies make for longer survival.

Implicit to this transformation of the body from an object geared to the rigors of nature to one defined by its fit to the made modern world is a new, culturally driven view of the body. The body is now not simply a natural "given" but a form of personal property, an object one owns and is responsible for maintaining and developing. Nor are such maintenance and development merely a matter of individual choice. There is a clear, if unspoken, underlying ideology of the contemporary body that is directly in line with the values represented in all the other creations of modernity: planes, trains, automobiles, and, most conspicuously, buildings. Indeed, the slogan of modern Bauhaus architecture, "Form follows function," and the buildings designed by Frank Lloyd Wright, with their clean lines and exposed construction materials, can serve as an unmistakable template for the modern body.

The industrial age also brought with it the idealization of efficiency and rationality. The efficiency of any machine is defined by its energy input to output ratio and its power to weight ratio. This ideal can be achieved only through applying rationality, in the form of mechanical engineering. Like the ideal machine, the efficiency of the modern body requires excess weight to be shed, and the means to accomplish this are provided by the rationality of biomedical and nutrition science. And so it is no mere whim of fashion that conjures up a lean, streamlined human body as the modern ideal but, rather, a blend of the fundamental values associated with modernity. Nothing, however, is more contradictory of those values than obesity. Immersed in a culture dedicated almost everywhere to the achievement of light, slim, energy-efficient design, how could we not apply these criteria to ourselves?

But having applied them, we encounter one of the paradoxes of modern life. The same conditions of relative affluence and freedom from the hazards of nature that technology provides for us also make it very difficult for us to avoid obesity. It is all too obvious that, while many of our objects (telephones, televisions, computers, and so on) have steadily grown slimmer, our bodies have not. On the one hand, surrounded on all sides by energy-saving devices, we lack the everyday, calorie-burning activities that once helped prevent obesity. On the other hand, surrounded by an ever-growing variety of foods and drinks from all over the world, many of which have been carefully designed and marketed to tantalize our appetites, we are more and more easily seduced into the overindulgence that makes for obesity. The way out of this paradox that began to emerge in North America during the 1920s and is still with us is dieting.

Studies of American eating patterns have shown that, by the late 1920s and on into the Depression years of the '30s, dieting had become a major cultural movement, particularly among middle- and upper-class women. This occurred despite the fact that at the same time, large numbers of working-class

Americans were going hungry or were malnourished because of the economic depression. Although the various fad diets that were and are still followed made their primary appeal on the basis of aesthetics, this was quickly augmented by appeals to health. At the end of the 19th century, fad diets claiming to provide not only beauty but also new or renewed health and energy had begun to circulate in the U.S. It was only after World War I, however, that the effects of urbanization, science education, fashion changes promoted in the mass media, and the progress of modern medicine combined to popularize the idea of dieting for the sake of health and attractiveness. By the 1930s, the medical evidence against obesity was increasing, and it has accumulated ever since. Yet the only serious solutions to the obesity problem offered by the medical and nutrition sciences are dieting and exercise, solutions which, for the vast majority of people who wish to be thin, do not work.

They don't work because the facts of physiology and psychology work against them. Those who study dieting have noted that the physics of weight gain are such that, if you average merely fifty calories a day over the amount of energy you expend through exercise, you will gain ten pounds in the course of a year. At the same time, the psychological pressures and temptations in favor of eating and against exercising are very strong and, in certain respects, almost unavoidable. Even when people are able to rigorously adhere to a diet and exercise program that results in significant weight loss, they typically regain the lost weight as they relax their adherence to the program. This is because of a combination of psychological and physiological factors. The psychology is quite obvious: people usually begin diet-exercise programs when their motivation is at a high peak, because of either disgust at their flabby looks or dire health warnings from a physician, or both. For most people, the initial high level of motivation has nowhere to go but down, and after several weeks of effort, any number of life events will cause their motivation to drop. People may become frustrated or depressed at the lack of dramatic weight loss; they may experience painful muscle strain or injury from exercising; work or family demands may interfere with the routine; health fears may wane; and any one of all the usual personal problems that can come up may lead to frustration and depression.

Depression is the most potent of the emotional forces preventing weight loss and, worse, encouraging weight gain. Clinical case histories frequently show that overeating is a common response to any form of social loss or rejection that can leave one feeling unloved or unworthy. As therapists have described it, this emotional pattern in which food consumption serves as a surrogate for love or comfort originates in early childhood, when mother love and nurturance are identical with feeding. As a result, eating, and especially overeating, often persists later in life as the most immediate way to compensate for depression or loss of love. A powerful illustration of this process is frequently found in the case histories of women who have been seriously abused by their boyfriends or spouses. Overeating provides a form of emotional compensation while at the same time increasing their physical ability to resist abuse.

So there are several major and minor psychological conditions that tend to erode the willpower one needs to resist the temptations of overeating and physical inactivity. And these conditions help explain not only why people do not persist in their weight control efforts—it is estimated that 50 percent of those in exercise programs drop out within six months—but also why most people never begin them. Surveys indicate that approximately 70 percent of North Americans do not exercise regularly. The dieting data are equally dismal. Estimates are that, among those who enroll in formal diet plans, 50 to 75 percent drop out within a few months. Among those who stay on a plan, about half regain their lost weight within a few years.

Insidious as they may appear, the psychological forces ranged against effective dieting are at least straightforward, compared with inherited physiological factors. First among these is metabolism. Those adults who apparently can eat anything in almost any quantity and yet remain fashionably thin throughout most of their lives are invariably people who were born with high metabolisms. They simply burn off calories at a much faster rate than the rest of us. At the other extreme are those born with low and slow metabolisms, those who often say they gain weight just by *looking* at food. More to the point of dieting, though, is the relatively obscure and somewhat controversial fact—controversial because it does not occur consistently in everyone—that, when there is a significant decrease in the amount of food eaten, the body reduces its metabolic rate to conserve energy. The longer we persist in eating less, the more difficult it becomes to lose weight. This is why burning up calories with exercise is such an important component of any dieting program. When food consumption returns to its normal level, however, metabolism speeds up to its normal level. Like it or not, our metabolism acts as an automatic weight-balancing mechanism. To defeat this mechanism and reduce cravings for food, some people turn to drugs.

The most effective of the various diet drugs available are amphetamines, or "uppers" in street lingo. These drugs speed up metabolism and suppress appetite, but they also disturb sleep-waking patterns, induce brittle emotional states, and can cause cardiac problems. And with the passage of time, they lose their potency unless taken in increasing doses. Professional dancers and other performers who fear that loss of a slim figure will harm their careers are notorious for becoming addicted. Judy Garland and Marilyn Monroe were two of the more famous examples. It has been estimated that approximately 14 percent of women on diets in the early 1990s were using some form of appetite-suppressant pills.

As well as establishing our metabolism, genetics may influence our body weight by determining the number of fat cells we are likely to develop. Some research indicates that fat cells develop if we eat too much during early childhood, and it is believed that the number of fat cells in the body cannot be reduced later on in life. Childhood obesity, therefore, is considered a predictor of adult obesity. Since clinical case histories suggest that mothers with guilt or anxiety concerning their children tend to overfeed them to compensate, it seems that here again our weight problems may be traced to our parents: they are responsible either for passing on obesity-inducing genes or for overfeeding, or both.

These interwoven social, biological, and psychological forces promoting obesity explain why the problem is so obstinate. There is hardly any aspect of modern life that is not conducive to weight gain. An important consequence of this is that more and more people are unhappy about their bodies. Surveys conducted by the magazine *Psychology Today* indicate a steady rise in this complaint. In 1972, 35 percent of men and 48 percent of women were dissatisfied with their body weight. By 1985, 41 percent of men and 55 percent of women said they were dissatisfied, and this trend apparently continued into the '90s. People's ongoing and increasing unhappiness with their bodies sustains a huge dieting industry, as well as fitness centers and personal trainers for those who can afford them. It is also a primary factor underlying the problem of anorexia and bulimia among young women, and among a small but increasing number of young males in the affluent societies of Western Europe, North America, and Japan.

Epidemiology studies show that these disorders are found mainly among teenage girls and young adult women from middle- and upper-class families. Before the late 1950s, anorexia and bulimia were considered rare medical curiosities, but, starting in the '60s, their prevalence steadily increased. By the 1970s, one study found that approximately 10 percent of Swedish high school girls had experienced the symptoms of anorexia, and in 1981 researchers at a New York university reported that 13 percent of female students were bulimic, having more than once binged and then induced vomiting. A 1990 summary of the problem concluded that, by the late 1980s, eating disorders had become one of the most common health problems among young women on U.S. college campuses and were particularly frequent at the more prestigious schools.

Because of their historical novelty, the absence of any clear-cut physiological causes, and their life-threatening effects, anorexia and bulimia have provoked a variety of explanations. These range from psychological and cultural analyses to psychiatric interpretations. Both the data concerning social class and the psychiatric evidence present tantalizing challenges to theorists. Why should these disorders occur primarily among relatively privileged young women? And why should those who are afflicted typically develop distorted perceptions of their bodies, seeing themselves as fat when they are actually drastically underweight or emaciated?

The findings suggest that young women at the upper end of affluent societies are more sensitive than others to cultural ideals that emphasize slimness as a feature of feminine beauty. Moreover, surveys and case histories indicate that it is the most competitive and achievement-oriented teenage girls who are at the greatest risk. This is why most psychiatrists and social theorists see anorexia and bulimia as ideology disorders — manifestations of the young woman's drive to achieve perfection through her body, just as she may be attempting to achieve it through schoolwork, sports, and social skills. Anorexics tend to excel in these areas. And their participation in sports and concern with fashionable clothing are noteworthy because both involve an implicit or explicit focus on competition. They encourage objectification of the body: a view of the body as an object that requires attention and discipline lest it get out of control, becoming "fat" and no longer competitive. Beneath the drive to attain the beauty ideal of slimness, therefore, is the more significant issue of self-esteem. According to this view, having a slim body is not the real goal; it is merely the stepping-stone toward high self-esteem. If excessive body weight were the cultural ideal, young women concerned with self-esteem would strive to gain weight rather than lose it.

A feminist variation on the theme of self-esteem highlights sexism. The theory is largely based on the fact that anorexia and bulimia often originate when the bodies of teenage girls are beginning to become noticeably different from the bodies of teenage boys. For the competitive young high-achiever, the advent of menstruation and larger breasts can be experienced both as a loss of control ("my body is changing out from under me") and as stigmata indicating the arrival of womanhood. To the extent that women are perceived, correctly or incorrectly, to have a lower social status than men and fewer opportunities to pursue desirable careers, the ambitious teenager may see her transformation to womanhood as a sign of impending inferiority. In this context, anorexia and bulimia can be understood as struggles against sexism and the losses associated with maturation. A starvation diet will delay menstruation and further development of secondary sex characteristics, thereby preventing movement into the threatening status of womanhood.

The more straightforward psychiatric approaches to eating disorders are usually traced to the pioneering work of psychiatrist Hilde Bruch in the 1970s. Based on her clinical experience treating anorexics, Bruch suggested that their problems with food were rooted in a conflict between their desire to satisfy the high-achievement values of their relatively affluent families and their feelings of inadequacy or fears of failure. But why should this lead to an eating disorder? In most families it doesn't. There are many ways, some quite healthy and others rather neurotic, for teenagers to work out their anxieties about achievement other than developing an eating disorder. Boys, for example, are likely to engage in overt rebellious activities, whereas girls may rebel less openly by deliberately allowing their schoolwork to deteriorate, or through sexual promiscuity. And both boys and girls can become immersed in fantasies, experiment with drugs, or, in extreme cases, run away from home.

But in situations where such common forms of adolescent rebellion are not feasible—where a teenage girl lacks the confidence to act out, where her fragile sense of self-esteem depends on the approval she receives for good grades, and where the atmosphere at home has sensitized her to the importance of slim physical attractiveness—an eating disorder is much more likely to develop. According to Bruch, the classic situation making teenage girls more susceptible to anorexia or bulimia goes like this: one or both parents are successful high-achievers with high aspirations for their children. The parents consistently take pains with their personal appearance and may frequently make critical remarks about those who do not. There is also a strong family emphasis on personal discipline and being in control.

For the maturing teenage girl in this family who comes to feel a frightening loss of control as she gains weight en route to womanhood, and who is exposed to the peer pressures of dating and physical attractiveness, and who may be teased about her appearance, dieting will appear to be an entirely appropriate, emotionally satisfying course of action. But dieting is not easy for a youngster surrounded by readily available, tempting treats. It requires a strong effort of will, exactly the sort of personal discipline valued by her parents. And so it appears to her that, if she can resist eating, she will be on her way to improving her appearance, gaining the approval of peers and parents, and demonstrating to herself that she has what it takes—personal discipline—to be in control of her life. Her conclusion: the only thing standing in the way of happiness and success is eating.

Food becomes the enemy: the ugly, threatening demon that must be overcome. The mere sight of food can invoke anxiety and a self-disgust that can bring on nausea.

This full-scale anorexic response to food does not develop overnight. It may begin simply with avoiding certain foods, and by skipping a meal, usually breakfast or lunch. It becomes more serious when there is a relapse from such rational, if unwise, dieting. Usually in moments of fatigue or depression, appetite cravings overcome inhibitions and plunge the person into a binge in which many of the tempting foods that she has carefully avoided are eaten in a minor orgy of sensual pleasure. This can provide the opening for bulimia to enter as the way station toward anorexia. As with all other binges, the food binge is invariably followed by feelings of guilt, and for this there is the perfect solution. By throwing up what has been consumed, the bulimic can eliminate evidence of the relapse and, at the same time, reduce her feelings of guilt through the penance or self-punishment of vomiting. This allows the bulimic to have her cake and eat it too, while maintaining a sense of righteousness.

Anorexia is not always preceded by bulimia, and it is estimated that many more young women remain bulimic rather than progressing into anorexia. The movement to anorexia occurs when eating anything at all brings about a high level of anxiety and becomes a direct threat to self-esteem. This behavior pattern is strengthened by what therapists refer to as the secondary gains of anorexia. The primary gain, of course, is weight loss and movement toward the ideal of slimness. But, especially in its formative stage, extreme dieting behaviors provide the teenager or young adult with substantial secondary social-emotional rewards. At the more obvious level, there is praise and admiration from friends and family for her discipline and improved figure. And since anorexics are often likely to adopt intensive exercise programs or take part in competitive sports such as tennis or distance running, they will also receive praise for their devotion to a workout routine or sports training. But at a less obvious and sometimes unconscious level, there is likely to be a satisfying sense of power achieved through the gain of passive aggression. At first, this sense of power comes from the simple refusal to participate in familiar patterns of eating with family and friends, and seems understandable as an act of rational self-improvement. It is apparently innocuous and nonthreatening to pass up sharing in pizzas, burgers, desserts, or whatnot, but may already be the beginning of an implicit rejection of the social values involved in eating together with others. To refuse to eat what "they" are eating, or to not join in eating at all, is to separate oneself from "them." As the refusal to share in conventional eating patterns becomes more consistent, the anorexic's behavior is likely to become a source of increasing anxiety to others. And so the anorexic becomes a center of attention and concern, which reinforce her sense of importance and demonstrate the power of her self-assertion over eating to influence those around her.

The anorexic's rejection of food has its strongest aggressive impact on family members, particularly mothers, when weight loss reaches the point of becoming an unmistakable threat to health. As mentioned earlier, infant feeding is considered to be the embodiment of mother love, and the food mothers prepare for their growing (and grown-up) children continues to be an important expression of their love. When a mother's food is rejected—even if it is only take-out she ordered over the telephone—and this rejection goes on long enough to affect the health of her daughter, she will grow increasingly worried and upset. Some psychiatric theorists see this situation as the anorexic daughter's ultimate act of passive-aggressive rebellion or revenge against her mother. Revenge for what? It can be any number of things but typically is thought to involve the mother's excessive efforts to control her daughter or bind her daughter to her own needs and ambitions. In this interpretation, anorexia is understood as resulting from a daughter's resistance to a mother who has been treating her daughter as a surrogate for herself—someone who will fulfill ambitions that she, the mother, could not accomplish in her own life. Interestingly, in her treatment of anorexics, Bruch found that their mothers were often women who had put aside their careers to raise a family.

Fathers are not absolved, however. Case histories of anorexic young women frequently indicate that they identify strongly with their fathers and the "masculine" values such as assertiveness and self-discipline their fathers represent. In such instances, when the father is an attractive authority figure whose achievements set a standard that seems beyond the abilities of the teenage girl, she may, as suggested by some feminist writers, attribute her frustration to her feelings of being trapped in a female body. Radical dieting can serve as both a demonstration of strong, "masculine" self-discipline and a way of attaining a more masculine, slimmer body. It should be clear enough, then, that anorexia is what psychotherapists refer to as an overdetermined condition, usually following from the convergence of several social, psychological, and cultural factors, any one of which may be a sufficient cause.

While all the social and emotional rewards that initially result allow the anorexic to see the renunciation of eating as a rational way to gain self-esteem, the avoidance of eating sooner or later becomes an uncontrollable obsession. The anorexic begins to experience intense anxiety if she fails to maintain the self-starvation regime. This transformation of radical dieting to an obsessive-compulsive behavior seems to occur through self-imposed conditioning, a type of self-induced brainwashing. It is similar in principle to the way some behavior therapists try to help people quit smoking. Smokers are encouraged to acquire a negative gut reaction to cigarettes by visualizing their harmful effects. They are shown pictures of malignant lung tumors paired with cigarettes and exposed to dramatic accounts of painful death from lung cancer. They are taught to cope with temptations to smoke by adopting substitute behaviors, urged to focus attention on the health benefits of quitting smoking, and given suggestions of how to reward themselves for not smoking. When it works, this conditioning process creates a powerful aversion to cigarettes, and smoking is transformed from a pleasurable act to a source of threatening anxiety. Anorexics go through a process like this with eating, but they do it on their own, aided by the pervasive cultural emphasis on the attractions of slimness, the ugly stereotypes of fatness, and praise from others for their weight loss. And the self-esteem gained from radical dieting can serve as an important prop supporting the teenager's sense of independent identity. The final result of this hard-won aversion to eating is a reflexive negative reaction to the mere thought of eating.

Once anorexic behavior of the caliber described here has become firmly established, it is very resistant to change. Like serious smoking addicts and alcoholics, anorexic and bulimic young women may complete treatment programs that appear to alleviate their problem, but they remain highly vulnerable to relapses in times of stress. Nevertheless, treatment can be effective, particularly when it involves both behavior modification and insight counseling. These procedures used to modify behavior are designed to desensitize the young woman to her self-induced fear of eating. Usually applied in a hospital or clinic setting, they first try to weaken and then reverse the conditioned food-aversion reflex. Keeping the patient in a controlled environment where all the prior rewards associated with weight loss are no longer available facilitates this. The only major gain or reward available is release from the institution, and this is convincingly presented as possible only if the patient eats at a normal level again. As eating increases, she receives small-scale rewards, including opportunities to ventilate anxieties and related issues of self-esteem, and to gain insight through sessions with a sympathetic counselor or therapy group. Both counterconditioning and counseling help the patient change her behavior.

An alternative treatment also reported to be successful is based on changing the family dynamics associated with the problem. Developed as a form of family therapy by the Italian therapist M.S. Palazolli, this approach requires parents to participate in procedures designed to eliminate the source of their daughter's need to struggle for self-esteem and control by not eating. The fundamental premise is that the girl and her parents have become enmeshed in an intensely emotional struggle, a struggle that can be abated by having both parties grant each other a greater degree of autonomy. This requires the parents to relinquish many of their efforts to shape their daughter's behavior and to recognize her need to develop an independent sense of identity. Briefly, the reasoning here is that, when allowed to explore an expanding range of developmental possibilities beyond those defined by her immediate family, the daughter will no longer need to avoid food, having found more appropriate ways to enhance her self-esteem and relate to her parents.

These descriptions of treatments for anorexia and bulimia may create a false impression about the practical effectiveness of therapy. In all too many cases, the therapeutic procedures can fail or fall short of their objective because they are not applied properly, because they are stopped prematurely, or because the patients and their families may be too resistant. Successful treatment is also difficult because of the overdetermination problem. Since various social, psychological, and cultural factors contribute to the onset of these eating disorders, they do not yield easily to treatment and are prone to reappear even years after remission. In this respect, the eating-aversion disorders, like other addictive problems, including the overeating associated with obesity, all show a similar resistance to treatment.

The most striking parallel between the problems of overeating and undereating is their apparent common origin in feelings of low self-esteem brought on by emotions associated with stress, anxiety, and depression, as I discussed at the beginning of this chapter. Overeating is by far the most frequent way people comfort themselves in the face of these emotional states. This is because the consumption of feel-good foods is so closely linked to childhood experiences of love. (Not for nothing do we have the aphorism "The way to a man's heart is through his stomach.") But in more severe circumstances, when negative feelings are very intense, appetite often disappears. During periods of acute stress, when the body is geared for fight or flight behavior, hunger evaporates. And for different reasons, the same thing can happen when people are deeply immersed in grief and depression following the death of a loved one. In general, these situations suggest that while eating offers effective compensation for moderate levels of distress—overeating can smother anxiety and depression if they are not too extreme—it fails when the negative emotions reach very high levels.

Less extreme than the problems described above but no less interesting are the borderline or near-pathological food behaviors that fall short of being considered disorders. These idiosyncratic food habits, or eccentricities, also appear to originate as responses to stress, anxiety, or traumatic experiences. And although they are usually not associated with serious behavior problems or threats to health, they can create certain adjustment problems. A.W. Logue provides an outstanding illustration of this in her 1986 book on the psychology of eating and drinking. As a child, she claims, she ate only bread and milk. As a teenager, she refused any ethnic foods (including pizza and spaghetti), all fresh fruit except bananas, and most vegetables and ate only cheese if it was in a grilled-cheese sandwich. She concludes her list of aversions by remarking succinctly: "Fish I regarded as poison." None of this seems to have done her any harm, except on various social occasions when she had to contend with one or more of the items she couldn't tolerate.

As an adult, Logue did get over some of her food aversions. This was mainly due to the efforts of her husband, who managed to persuade her to eat fruit, vegetables, and some ethnic foods (but never fish). One can't help wondering about the origin of her wide range of aversions, which appears to have started in infancy or early childhood. But Logue offers no explanation except to say that her parents had unusual food preferences. Her mother disliked fresh fruit and fish, and hated liver, whereas her father enjoyed liver. At the dinner table, her father would habitually first eat the foods he disliked the most before moving on to those he liked better — an unusual behavior that must have contributed to the family atmosphere of food eccentricity.

No Freudian but rather a strict experimental research psychologist, Logue has nothing to say about the emotional patterns that might have been responsible for either her parents' food habits or her own. Yet even a conservative interpretation of her account suggests that she must have acquired her aversions early on from her mother. Since infants and young children are keenly sensitive to their mother's emotional states, it is hard to imagine that Logue would not have experienced some degree of vicarious anxiety over the foods her mother obviously disliked. Also, as discussed in the previous chapter, recent research demonstrates that infants are sensitive to the flavors in their mother's breast milk, which then become the basis for their initial food preferences. And since Logue grew up in a family where idiosyncratic food preferences were quite acceptable ("I come from a long line of people with unusual food preferences," she writes), there would have been little or no reason for her to relinquish her early food aversions. On the contrary, it seems likely that she would have gained some rewarding attention in the family by elaborating on her aversions as she grew up.

Logue's story is unusual because, much of the time, idio-syncratic food aversions result from easily understandable trau-matic or near-traumatic experiences. A classic example of this, described in chapter 2, is the incident involving Norman Dixon, who saw a schoolmate find a dead mouse in his por-ridge. It is a perfect illustration of what behavior-modification theorists call one-trial conditioning. A less extreme incident left my youngest son with a profound aversion to chicken that lasted several years. While visiting with my mother when he was four years old, he noticed the whole raw chicken she had bought for our dinner—the legs and feet sticking out from the wrapping. He was horrified at this discovery of the connection between a live chicken with its own feet and the dead thing in my mother's kitchen. He ran out of the kitchen shouting "little feet," and refused to accept any explanation we could offer about this being the same sort of packaged chicken he had often seen his own mother buy in the supermarket. It seemed clear that he felt as if he had suddenly fallen in with a group of canni-bals, and I recall thinking at the time that, in his innocence, he was not entirely wrong.

Many of the more common food aversions are not based on any dramatic experience but simply arise from the taste, smell, or appearance of the food. Children are particularly sensitive to these food qualities. I can still remember being disgusted at the pickled herring that was one of my father's favorite foods, although at some point as an adult I began to enjoy it myself. More elaborate food-preference studies invari-ably report that liver is the most widely disliked and avoided food in North America. This is readily understandable. Given its darkly pungent taste, smell, appearance, heaviness, and chewiness, liver presents itself to most children and many adults as especially ugly, primal, and repulsive—something that might be enjoyed by Conan the Barbarian. On the other hand, one of the best-liked foods in North America is pizza, which is everything that liver is not, being brightly colored, fragrant, and easy to chew while watching TV.

As indicators of near pathology, however, specific food aversions are often trivial compared with obsessive-compulsive eating habits. These habits are widely recognized by therapists as the most conspicuous demonstration of emotional anxieties being projected onto food. Although at the beginning of this chapter I noted that food pathologies fundamentally involve either eating too much or eating too little, obsessive-compulsive ways of eating might properly be added as the strongest indicator of near pathology. Some common examples of such food behaviors have already been mentioned. Others include careful searching through the contents of any dish before eating, lest it contain something suspicious; separating diverse items on a plate so they don't touch each other; eating only the most or least preferred items first; and less noticeable habits such as always adding salt, pepper, or ketchup to food before tasting it.

Then there are food fetishes or rituals, often based on ethnic, religious, or health beliefs. Many older Catholics, for example, were raised to believe that they should not eat meat on Fridays and today persist in this ritual even though the church no longer requires it. An Orthodox Jew will refuse any meal containing a mixture of meat and dairy products and will eat meat only from animals that have been slaughtered according to certain ritual procedures. (An Orthodox Jew in my basic training company many years ago had a hard time in the army because he was unable to eat the nonkosher food, even though the Jewish chaplain said this was permitted.) There are dedicated North American vegetarians and Indian Brahmins who share a distaste, if not horror, at the thought of consuming meat, or, in the case of vegans, consuming any animal product at all. Finally, there are those who believe that certain dietary practices are essential for health. Some will drink only distilled water, or bottled water from a particular source, or maybe any sort of water so long as they have at least seven glassfuls each day. Others believe that better health can be achieved by chewing each mouthful of food at least twenty-five or fifty times before swallowing, or that they should purify their digestive system by fasting once a week, or twice a month. And still others follow more elaborate food regimes, such as the macrobiotic diet, which is supposed to keep the body properly balanced in accord with the yin and yang principles of Chinese philosophy.

This list of obsessive-compulsive practices and fetishes is by no means exhaustive; whole books have been devoted to the subject. Nor is it my intent to argue that these food practices are in themselves dysfunctional. On the contrary, in many instances, there is respectable evidence showing that they may be quite sensible. The central point, however, is that such practices frequently are adopted by people who are trying to find ways of coping with neurotic anxieties directly or indirectly related to food.

Anxieties directly related to food are almost always traceable back to childhood experiences, and most of them involve relationships between children and their mothers. Consequently, and despite the risk of being accused of "mother-bashing," it seems clear that, since mothers are the primary source of feeding and nurturance, they are also very likely to be the source of anxieties leading to unusual eating habits in their children. The mother who constantly worries that her child may put something dirty in his or her mouth, or insists on wiping her child's mouth clean of food residue after every mouthful, or tries to prevent her child from picking up food in his or her hands, is conditioning the child to associate food with anxiety. For the child, every occasion of eating becomes fraught with the likelihood that he or she will do something wrong or messy and be corrected or scolded. This is the sort of pattern that can produce adults who are overly concerned with clean utensils and making sure that nothing "wrong" or "dirty" passes their lips.

At the opposite extreme is the mother who is indifferent and excessively permissive about feeding her child. In this case, the child may be left too much on his or her own when dealing with food. The child may then feel confused or overwhelmed by the uncertainties associated with eating. Unsupervised and guided only by impulses, the child's spontaneous manner of eating can cause choking or regurgitation when he or she tries to swallow too much at one time, or hunger when the inattentive mother removes the food before the child has had enough. The anxiety that develops will be focused on the potential disorderliness and risky ambiguities of eating, predisposing the child-as-grown-up to impose order and eliminate ambiguities. The child may become the adult who compulsively arranges the food on the plate or systematically eats only one item at a time.

But mothers should not be held responsible for everything that can create anxiety about eating. The distinct digestive system and sensitivities of each child in the same family can vary a great deal; the same food experience enjoyed by one can cause problems for another. And those children with undiagnosed allergies or other physiological problems may already at a very young age begin to experience mild to severe discomfort after eating. If this occurs frequently enough, it can easily become the basis for an association between eating and anxiety, particularly when facing novel or unfamiliar foods. A well-recognized case in point concerns people who are allergic to MSG (monosodium glutamate), a preservative and flavor enhancer often used in Chinese and other restaurants. Because they can suffer traumatic allergic reactions, those who have this sensitivity learn to be obsessively cautious when eating out, and many restaurants will note on their menus that MSG is present in certain dishes. And so a good deal of both theory and common experience indicates that many obsessive-compulsive or eccentric food behaviors are rooted in overcontrolling or indifferent mothering, or in various sorts of physiological sensitivities. But there are other, less direct, routes toward obsessive eating habits that can emerge in adults who, as children, had no difficulties with food.

In some instances, such as among people who develop paranoid fears of persecution, food or water can become one of the focal points for their anxieties. An extreme example appears in the classic film *Dr. Strangelove*, in which a paranoid air force general who launches an attack against the Soviet Union drinks only distilled water because he believes that his sexual impotence is due to drinking tap water that has been adulterated by Communist agents. A mild form of this "contamination" theme is exploited in the merchandising of bottled water and home water-purification devices. The popularity of these products is at least partly due to the fact that water is a very convenient object on which to project a wide range of greater or lesser anxieties. Unfortunately, this sort of fear is occasionally supported by news reports of unsafe water supplies. Another variation on water paranoia occurred during the 1950s and '60s, when there were bitter conflicts in many communities over water fluoridation. Despite all assurances from health authorities that it was safe and helped prevent tooth decay, some people remained convinced that fluoride in the water might have dangerous side effects.

Aside from water, there are enough widely publicized reports of occasionally contaminated meats and chicken (with bovine spongiform encephalopathy, causing Creutzfeldt-Jakob [mad cow] disease, in Europe; with *E. coli* bacteria in the U.S.) to support the fears of anyone inclined toward food anxieties. Nor are fruits and vegetables entirely innocent: insecticides used during cultivation and preservatives applied before shipment provide a substantial basis for anxiety. (Some authorities assert that apples should be peeled before eating, and all produce should be washed in decontaminating solutions.) And I know people who avoid salad bars in restaurants and supermarkets because, as they say, "Who knows what germs or other stuff may have been left in them by careless children or ill or dirty people." In general, since any of these food fears may some-times be justified, they provide a plausible basis for some people to maintain high levels of anxiety over what they eat. An extreme and clearly neurotic case is the food behaviors of billionaire Howard Hughes. During the last several years of his life, he trusted only a small group of Mormon men employed as his servants. They supervised the preparation of his meals by a specially selected cook and were required to wear immaculate white gloves and surgical masks when serving him.

By way of conclusion, perhaps the most appropriate thing to emphasize about the food pathologies and near-pathological eccentric eating behaviors discussed in this chapter is that they are a growing problem in our society precisely at a time when, by all objective accounts, we have the safest and most diversified food supplies in history. The irony is evident and speaks directly to the fact that psychological meanings of food often have little or no connection with nutrition science or other "objective" facts. Instead, it seems that the very proliferation and ubiquity of food in our society are what stimulate the growth of the major pathologies—obesity, anorexia, and bulimia—and the various minor or near pathologies.

A persuasive explanation for this state of affairs can be drawn from the Marxist discussion of the contrast between the "use" value of any object and its "exchange" value. As it applies to food, this suggests that, since it is readily available in our society, food's use value for the satisfaction of hunger and nutritive needs is easily taken for granted and trivialized, whereas its symbolic or exchange value becomes increasingly prominent. More concretely, the mere satisfaction of hunger becomes secondary to the functions that food can serve as a status symbol or a sign of sophistication, aesthetic sensitivity, love and affection, or ethnic, religious, or even political convictions. When the labor leader Cesar Chavez was organizing Mexican farmworkers in California in the 1960s and '70s, for example, those sympathetic to the cause—"*la raza*"—were urged to boycott grapes, because grape growers were targeted as exploiters of labor. A person's political views could then be inferred from whether or not he or she continued to eat grapes.

Clearly, to the extent that a particular food is expensive, difficult to prepare, or just difficult to get, its exchange value will be much greater than its use value. The social-psychological significance of caviar, for example, is far out of proportion to its ability to satisfy hunger. This principle suggests that the prevalence of eating pathologies in our affluent society is closely connected to the increasing importance we have placed on the social and emotional exchange value of food.

CHAPTER 4

The McDonaldization of Taste

M OST, IF NOT ALL, of our common knowledge about food and the ways we relate to it is dictated by one or more of three distinctively different food ideologies. Like political ideologies (Communism, Fascism), food ideologies influence how we think, and try to persuade us how we *ought* to think, about their subject matter. As systems of related ideas and principles of action, these ideologies not only mediate our behavior but also drape their subject matter with myths, metaphors, and assumptions that prevent purely reflexive experiences. It would seem impossible, for example, for someone raised as an Orthodox Jew or Muslim to have an unmediated experience with a pork chop or ham sandwich because he or she would inevitably feel some sense of guilt, or at least an awareness of violating a religious prohibition. It is also unlikely that most North Americans could have an unmediated experience eating fried grasshoppers, puppy dogs, or horse meat. But why?

The usual commonsense answer would appeal to the cultural conditioning and social norms that define appropriate foods for people in various societies and ethnic groups. This is certainly not wrong, so far as it goes. The answer to be elaborated in this chapter, however, goes somewhat deeper. It proposes that everywhere, and in all human groups, our thinking and behaviors about food are in one way or another dictated by the ideologies of hedonism, nutritionism, and spiritualism. In the example of the Jew and Muslim, it is clearly their spiritual (religious or metaphysical) ideology that is triggered by pork. And most of us are not inclined to try grasshoppers, dog meat, or horse meat because they are not seen as either pleasurable or nutritious, and to eat them would seem somewhat immoral.

More specifically, I will argue that much of the meaning we attribute to food can to a large extent be understood as emerging from the meeting of these three ideologies. As general systems of thought, they coexist rather uneasily and in fluctuating patterns of conflict within each one of us. Any time we look at a menu, shop for groceries, or hesitate in a cafeteria line, elements of the three ideologies are, whether consciously or not, probably competing with one another. A useful analogy can be drawn from Freudian theory, whereby our hedonistic desires for sensory pleasure reside in the id, concerns about health and nutrition in the ego, and spiritual, religious, or moral meanings in the superego. Depending on our circumstances, any one of these ideologies may become dominant, though most food behaviors tend to follow from some combination of hedonism and nutritionism.

The concept of hedonism is typically traced back to the early-19th-century work of philosopher Jeremy Bentham, who formulated a "hedonic calculus," which maintained that the overriding principle of life is to maximize pleasure and minimize pain, or even further back to the ancient (300 B.C.) Greek Epicureans. Where food is concerned, hedonism is an ideology that reduces the meaning of food to sensory pleasure. The driving motive here is appetite: visceral desire for the delicious gratifications of good taste experiences. But good taste is not everything. The ideology of hedonism also involves an aesthetics of food, with many items taking on the properties of an object of art and stimulant of desire. This can be seen most dramatically in gourmet magazines and books, with their lavish photos of specialty dishes and the implements used in their preparation and consumption—processing machines that could be space vehicles, cutlery worthy of a modern operating room. To see this arrayed alongside close-ups of sauces, soufflé, and swatches of pink flesh is to recognize that one is immersed in a display of rampant sensuality. In many ways, such layouts represent the pinnacle of food hedonism. The meats and fish lack only black stockings and red garter belts to complete the impression of sexual voyeurism. Much of the text accompanying the pictures supports this view. The metaphors and themes of narrative tension—cooking as foreplay, eating as consummation—and the rhythms of the writer's voice are all but perfectly reminiscent of sexual vernacular. Equally striking are the performers: mustachioed Latin chefs urging surrender to the pleasures of the palate, gossip columnists of cuisine with cute nicknames. They take on the role of impresarios whose stock in trade is the goading of jaded appetites.

Noteworthy too is that, unlike the competing food ideologies of nutritionism and spiritualism, which ignore social class differences, the hedonism displayed in gourmet magazines often celebrates it, virtually proclaiming itself an important criterion of social class. Not only are these magazines themselves relatively expensive to purchase, but also the advertisements and features in them seem aimed at people living on no less than

$100,000 a year. A good deal of what these magazines contain has as much to do with style as it does with actual food. Upper-class dining, as distinct from working-class eating, requires considerable specialized knowledge. As culture critic Paul Fussell has observed, "uppers" do not have paper napkins or bottles of ketchup on their tables, they never serve instant coffee, and they eat dinner at eight or nine o'clock, rather than at five-thirty or six, in order to have plenty of time for their cocktail hour.

Nevertheless, like most robust ideologies, food hedonism is a big tent that can accommodate anyone, regardless of social class. And no one knows this better than McDonald's, with its play areas, clowns, and Walt Disney figures. Here and at other fast-food outlets, the gross sensuality of the food is matched by the entertainments designed to attract children and the conveniences provided for their parents. The plebeian level of food hedonism can also be found in daily newspaper features and supermarket magazines devoted to what might be called "blue-collar cuisine"—that is, an endless variety of recommendations and recipes for inexpensive dishes that can be prepared easily by harried housewives and working mothers. At this level, hedonism is often accompanied by elements of nutritionism. Recipe introductions, for example, may include remarks about how to disguise healthy ingredients ("This is a great way to get your husband and children to enjoy broccoli").

The traditional ideological antagonist of hedonism is the spiritual ideology of food found in the major religions and many of the so-called cults. Judaism, Christianity, Islam, Hindu-ism, and Buddhism all warn against overindulgence in hedonis-tic pleasures of the flesh. Instead, they emphasize spiritual,

moral ideals of virtue based on restrictive diets or abstinence.
As touched upon in chapter 2, Catholics consider overeating
of any kind (gluttony) a venial sin; the Orthodox Jewish laws
governing kosher ("purity") foods warn against eating pork and
any meat from animals not slaughtered according to ritual procedures, as well as a number of other animal products. Muslims
also are forbidden to eat pork; many Buddhist sects specify total
vegetable and grain diets; and, among Hindus, meat products
are forbidden to the higher castes, and some Brahmins go further by adhering to only minimal vegetarian diets. Although
anthropologists and historians of cuisine point out that many
of these dietary practices may have originated in primitive
tribal groups as intuitive health measures or for ecological reasons (pigs can be carriers of trichinosis, and they do not thrive
in deserts), the persistence of these food traditions and their
link with spiritual and moral values clearly indicate the need for
a psychological explanation. How is it that certain foods and
eating practices can embody spiritual and moral values?

A number of explanations are plausible, but all of them
center on the one assertion that all religions have in common,
namely that humans are supposed to be different from, and
superior to, animals. The preeminent basis for this idea as well
as its "proof" is in our food behaviors. Unlike the animals,
including higher mammals, our eating practices are not entirely
driven by instinct. To the extent that we clean, cook, and otherwise prepare food before eating it, and refrain from consuming
certain foods that may be instinctively appealing, we elevate
ourselves above the animals. And so specific food practices can
be found at the root of all religions because they provide a set of
daily behavior standards which allow us humans to consistently

validate our superior status. Of course, these standards take on different forms in different groups living in different environments, but the central premise appears to be universal. By abstaining from certain potential food items (generally human flesh, certain animal flesh, sundry rodents and bugs), and by preparing other foods according to ritualized procedures (offering prayers or sacrifices, using certain cooking methods), humans create a tangible foundation for their sense of superiority. And the approved foods themselves begin to take on symbolic or metaphysical meanings that represent important moral and social values.

Once this premise is understood, the moral significance of food becomes easier to comprehend. To the extent that one masters instinctive animal drives and appetites for indiscriminate consumption, one rises to a higher level of human status, and a greater psychological separation is created between humans and animals. The ritual fasting, often followed by feasting, common to many religions is an instructive case in point: only humans do this. It is also instructive that a spartan or ascetic diet is almost always associated with the highest levels of spiritual and moral attainment and wisdom. Throughout history, those who have aspired to profound forms of spiritual experience, such as Native American shamans, Christian hermit monks, many of the saints, and the gurus of India, typically have undertaken prolonged fasting, presumably to facilitate mastery of the animal instincts that can block spiritual development. And most of the central figures portrayed in religious art appear rather underweight, though the big-bellied Buddha figures of Asia may be the exception. But this image can be explained by the fact that, in much of Asia, the lower abdomen is thought to be the center of vital body energy, known in Japan as *ki*, in China as *chi*. So in this case, the big belly has a special symbolic significance over and above food behavior.

In the West, plainness and simplicity are taken to be the hallmarks of morality. Among the Quakers, Amish, and other fundamentalist sects, this principle is applied not only to food but also to most other aspects of daily life. Any sort of excess, whether in speech, clothing, or elsewhere, is seen as immoral. Nevertheless, the sense of discipline and control that can protect one from the temptations of hedonism is based on dietary restraint, mastery of the visceral appetite. What better demonstration of this than the biblical story of Adam and Eve? Yielding to the temptation of the serpent's delicious-looking apple, Eve fails the obedience test in the Garden of Eden, and she and Adam are exiled forever. (Computer genius Steven Jobs take notice: no Bible scholar would have named his computer the Apple.)

We should not overlook the fact that food owes its traditional metaphysical significance to its being our indispensable source of life and well-being. In keeping with the moralistic concept of immanent justice (that bad things happen only to bad people), our primitive tribal ancestors took the availability of food as an unmistakable indicator of their spiritual status. If game was plentiful and harvests were good, then their gods were pleased with them. When their food supplies failed, the angry gods were punishing them for some wrongdoing. The origins of animal and human sacrifice aimed at pacifying the gods can be traced to this idea. A similar belief apparently accounts for certain religious rituals still followed in India, in which food offerings are made to Hindu deities.

There is no better way to summarize the spiritual and moral significance of food than by appealing to Mircea Eliade's *The Sacred and the Profane*, a classic work on the early history of human groups. Based on exhaustive study of religious myths, symbols, and rituals, Eliade concluded that almost any important bodily function could serve as a sacrament. Thus, the foods of our primitive ancestors were seen as gifts from the gods and, when eaten, were perceived as offerings to the gods of the body. This view of food is exactly what the modern science of dietetics and nutrition treats as mere superstition and has more or less succeeded in stamping out. On the authority of science, and in the name of modernity as well as the requirements and conveniences underpinning our contemporary lifestyles, nutritionism has succeeded in alienating most of us from the deeper metaphysics of food. Everyday experience, on the other hand, shows that nutritionism has not fared nearly as well in its struggle against hedonism.

To speak of nutrition science as an ideology, however, and to call it "nutritionism" is to be immediately at risk of being seen as a crackpot. Some defensive explanation is in order. Nutrition science, like all ideologies, is based on a causal theory about the human condition, in this case one stipulating that the biochemical properties of food determine health. And like all ideologies, nutritionism stipulates a method—the balanced diet—for putting its theory into practice. Nutrition science has been able to attain its status as a powerful ideology through a relatively straightforward process of abstraction. By thinking of all foods as being composed of a finite number of biochemical compounds called nutrients, and by breaking these down into their constituent components, all foods become, as it were, divided and conquered. The whole, regardless of whether it's lima beans or lobsters, rice pudding or lasagna, becomes no more than the sum of its parts. And those parts—the proteins, vitamins, minerals, and so on—that can be rigorously measured allow eating to become a quantitative bookkeeping operation in which the bottom line is a statistical invention known as the minimum daily requirement. This is an invention because it is based on averages compiled across vast numbers of people who are categorized only by gender. Differences in height, weight, metabolism, and other body processes are never mentioned in the tables listing our daily requirements.

Nutritionism is thus an ideology that as a matter of principle ignores all qualities of food except those relevant to conveniently measurable nutrients needed to produce energy. The common and most basic unit of analysis in nutrition science is, after all, the calorie, a measure of heat energy. Metaphorically, nutrition science conceptualizes food the way Victorian capitalist entrepreneurs conceived of their labor force: primarily in terms of the work or energy that can be extracted. But the critical factor allowing the science to be interpreted as an ideology is its promissory note to deliver health. Just as hedonism promises pleasure, and spiritualism promises a metaphysical or moral state of grace, nutritionism promises health. It does so by appealing to the authority of objective science as declared by the teachings of diverse health educators.

And so, the issue facing knowledgeable individuals in modern societies is whether to choose between the promises offered by the competing ideologies, or, much more commonly, to simply make an effort to get the best that each offers. But how can we get the best of three ideologies that are directly opposed to one another? Various studies of food habits show that people try to do this in many ways. From the results of my own research with college students, it is clear that most of them prioritize and compromise. When choosing what to eat, they typically emphasize hedonism, the pleasure or taste value of the food. The health and nutrition value runs a poor second, and spiritual or religious considerations hardly seem to exist at all, except among some vegetarians who mention both health and moral values. For vegetarians, nutritionism is clearly allied with spiritualism. There are also a few foods that are widely perceived as offering a good compromise between hedonism and nutritionism. Veggie pizza and chicken receive relatively high ratings for both pleasure and health.

Another type of compromise strategy older adults as well as college students follow is based on bargaining. This approach is mentioned frequently by the young women in my and my colleagues' studies. It involves skimping on or skipping a meal to justify indulgence in a rich dessert or some other hedonistic food. Then there is compromise based on trade-offs between meals. In one of our studies, students and older people generally agreed that their morning meal was the healthiest and their evening meal the most pleasurable. Lunch, however, was more of a catch-as-catch-can affair. Another not-too-surprising observation when comparing survey responses was that, as mentioned in chapter 2, middle-aged and older women place a greater emphasis on the health value of their meals than men or any other age group.

The results of our studies, and others as well, generally show that most people make their food choices in line with the ideologies of hedonism and nutritionism. And if the growing trend toward vegetarianism among young people continues to be encouraged by many of the celebrities they admire, we may yet see a resurgence of spiritualism. This ideology, including its conflicts with hedonism and nutritionism, was described eloquently by Mahatma Gandhi in his autobiography. His struggle with the three ideologies occurred at about age nineteen when he went to England to study law. Before this, while still in high school, Gandhi became convinced that his timidity and apparent weakness at sports could be cured by eating meat and bread instead of the rice and vegetable diet followed by his family. Some of his more self-assured friends even insisted that it was patriotic to eat meat, because this would provide them with the strength needed to liberate India from those meat-eating English! For a year he had occasional meat meals with his friends while feeling guilty about keeping this secret from his family. But, troubled by having to lie to his beloved mother, he gave this up. A few years later, when the time came for Gandhi to leave for England, his mother, fearful that her son would become corrupted among the British, made him take formal vows to resist the temptations of wine, women, and meat. He took these vows very seriously and stuck to them during his first months abroad, despite being pressured by both Indian and British friends to adopt the English diet.

But Gandhi had a miserable time of it trying to live on the few boiled vegetables available to him in a low-rent London boarding house, even with the supplements of sweets and spices mailed to him from India. This began to change when he discovered a few vegetarian restaurants in London and came across books extolling the virtues and health benefits of vegetarianism. He soon subscribed to the weekly newsletter of the British Vegetarian Society, met with some of its prominent members, and joined its executive committee. He describes having, in the course of his first year in England, something like an intellectual conversion that supported his spiritual commitment. On the one hand, he found some nutrition authorities endorsing the health benefits of vegetarianism. On the other hand, Gandhi became convinced of its ethical significance, in particular that humans should strive to live in harmony with nature, rather than trying to exploit it for their own advantage.

The effect of this perceived alliance between nutritionism and spiritualism turned Gandhi away from even the minimal hedonistic pleasures of vegetarianism. "The mind having taken a different turn," as he put it, Gandhi began to lose his desire for sweets and spicy vegetable dishes and came to enjoy simple things like boiled spinach. His dietary reflections close with the comment that he finally realized that the true source of our sense of taste is in the mind.

Gandhi's remark parallels Claude Lévi-Strauss's observation that what is "good to think" is good to eat. Yet it is also noteworthy that Gandhi's realization did not come easily. As a youth, he could not resist the potent temptations of meat, and as a young man, before his final conversion to vegetarianism, he consoled himself with traditional Indian sweets and spices. This developmental pattern of change is quite common. In a brief essay entitled "When a Man Is Small," M.F.K. Fisher, the renowned writer on cuisine, remarks on the typical changes in food preferences that occur as people grow to full maturity. According to Fisher, they are less driven by "ferocious" loves and hates for foods; judgment begins to temper desire, so that a more serious appreciation of food can develop. Teenagers, especially boys, will typically consume almost anything that tastes good to them, whereas older people become more cautious as their bodies become less tolerant of abuse. Fisher's remarks point to the fact that, as children and teenagers, our appetites are mainly dominated by the ideology of hedonism, whereas nutritionism begins to set in as we move into full adulthood.

In some of the research conducted with my colleagues, we found that young people generally become health or nutrition conscious for one of two reasons: training for sports, or as part of the responsibilities associated with marriage. Sports coaches and trainers can be important sources of nutrition information and attitude change, especially for young men. Among young adult women, however, we were surprised to find that, aside from their persistent concerns about weight loss, many of them began to shift from hedonism to nutritionism as they became committed to marriage. Despite the general climate of gender equality, many young women still accept the idea that they should be responsible for providing their husbands with nutritious meals, even if this only means eating fewer burgers and more veggie pizzas.

As a matter of common experience, it should be obvious also why hedonism becomes less attractive to people by the time they reach middle age. Nature, and the effects of self-indulgence, begin to catch up with most of us in our forties and fifties. These effects are usually strong enough to impose some degree of dietary restraint. Nothing can succeed in focusing our attention on nutrition and eating habits like the familiar mid-life health problems of hypoglycemia, kidney stones, gastritis, hypertension, or a mild heart attack, not to mention the sudden death of friends and other signals of our mortality. Hedonism is forced to go on the defensive, and the adage "All the foods we enjoy are bad for us" becomes commonplace. One of my colleagues now retired enjoys telling of how he arrived in the U.S. from Europe shortly after the end of World War II to attend college. He was astonished at the ready availability of meat, chocolate, and butter. These items were usually in short supply while he was growing up, so now he couldn't get enough of them. But later, in middle age, they became too much of a good thing. On doctor's orders, he gave up the treats and returned to something like his spartan wartime diet.

At middle age or a little later, there is also likely to be greater awareness of the spiritual significance of food. Many of the experiences—illness, the death of friends or parents—encouraging nutritionism may stimulate concerns about religion and morality as well. The convergence between nutritionism and spiritualism is most likely to be strongest among the elderly. Old age is the time when health problems and the inevitability of death become very real, and when appetites become less imperative. Changes in appetite are partly due to a dulling of taste sensitivity. Taste buds begin to atrophy, digestive processes become less robust, and chewing tasty foods is often difficult for those with dentures. Chronic illnesses and medications can also have adverse effects on taste sensitivity and appetite. Generally, as the physiological foundations for hedonism weaken, nutritionism and spiritualism begin to take over.

Reviewing the food habits of the elderly with my gerontology colleague George Peters, it also became clear that hedonistic cravings for special treats may be further reduced by psychological changes associated with memory. The youthful bliss experienced when consuming a milkshake, cheeseburger, or Mom's apple pie can be recalled, but it is rarely matched by today's pie or milkshake, not only because the items may not be the same but also because the keen desires and sensitivities of youthful appetite have faded. Nor is it simply a matter of appetite alone. The social and emotional context of eating plays a large role in how we respond to food, and, for many elderly people, this context is usually not nearly as vivid or stimulating as it is for younger people. On the contrary, even a favorite treat may be depressing if it triggers a memory of happy times that will never come again.

Concern with nutrition increases during old age not only because people become more aware of the bodily discomforts that can follow from indiscriminate eating but also because the elderly are frequently bombarded by advice about their eating habits from well-intentioned friends, relatives, and doctors. I have seen this take place in a local meal center where senior citizens may go to receive government-subsidized lunches. The meal itself is followed by a brief lecture on the necessity of a healthy diet, accompanied by recommendations of specific foods. Those who are homebound and receiving delivered meals are usually also given nutritional literature. In addition to this, many restaurant menus now list senior-citizen specials with a health (low fat and low salt) emphasis. And then there are the TV commercials in which elderly performers promote various products designed to reduce indigestion, increase regularity, or otherwise facilitate health. If the elderly in our society do not develop nutrition awareness on their own, it will usually be thrust on them.

Aging often comes with increased attention to the spiritual or religious significance of food. Gerontological research indicates that it is not unusual for older adults to spontaneously develop a keener sense of connection with nature, aroused probably by recognition that their life is coming to a close. Sometimes referred to as a feeling of "participation in the chain of nature," it often takes the form of heightened interest in gardening, birds, bees, and the various seasons and cycles of organic life. And it is apparently a general ecological sensitivity that often includes food in the chain of nature. There may even be the awareness I once heard explained by a retired physics professor, who said he had lately realized that eating is nothing more or less than a transfer of energy between two organic systems. Human consumers, in effect, are simply assimilating the energy contained in the animal or vegetable material on the plate in front of them.

When viewed from the chain-of-nature perspective, however, certain foods appear more representative of, or more closely connected with, the natural environment. Basic, relatively unprocessed, items that require little or no cooking, such as fruits and nuts, or staples such as cereals, rice, and beans, have this quality. A prime example of the elderly's bodily connection with nature via food is prunes. As simple as they are, prunes are directly connected with feelings of health or well-being. Since regular bowel movements are a preoccupation among many of the elderly, and since eating prunes is an effective way to accomplish this, the link between what grows in nature "out there" and digestive events "in here" can become very concrete.

Although aging may enhance the likelihood of a spiritual

orientation toward food, it is by no means a necessary prerequisite. That most religions have dietary rules has already been noted, but as Gandhi discovered in England, there is also a secular-humanist tradition emphasizing the moral and spiritual value of a simple vegetarian diet. This may seem like a contradiction to those who see secular humanism as equivalent to atheism, but it is often precisely those without any formal religious affiliation who feel the greatest need to assert their moral and spiritual values by adopting ascetic practices. ("If God does not exist, it is up to me to purify and redeem myself.") Much of the New Age concern with environmental and ecological issues is tied to the spiritual and ecological implications of food consumption, as may be seen in such popular books as *Diet for a New America* and *Small Is Beautiful*. The underlying theme here is that by eating lower down on the food chain (less meat, more grains and vegetables), one is carrying out a spiritual and moral act that will reduce pollution, help preserve ecological resources, and improve bodily health, thereby putting less strain on the health care system, and so on. What it comes down to is the conviction that, by having oatmeal instead of bacon and eggs for breakfast, you may or may not be doing God's work, but you are helping to save Earth and everyone on it.

The ideologies of spiritualism and nutritionism can be found most clearly intertwined in the formal principles of the macrobiotic food movement. According to the Ohsawa Foundation text *Zen Macrobiotics*, the macrobiotic movement was originally popularized through the works of George Ohsawa, a Japanese writer who developed a systematic philosophy of food consumption based on Buddhist concepts and the teachings of a 19th-century Japanese physician named Ishitsuka Sagen. Ohsawa's thesis was that the foundations of a healthy, meaningful life for individuals, and ultimately for whole societies, rest on appropriate food behaviors. Dedicated converts to the macrobiotic movement argue further that all the troubles of the modern world, from child abuse to wars, can be traced to our failures to appreciate the importance of food and cooking. Quite a sweeping statement on the face of it, but it rests on an elaborate analysis that follows from the familiar idea that we are what we eat.

Macrobiotic theory is grounded on the traditional Chinese principle that everything in the universe is essentially either yin or yang—feminine or masculine. The feminine yin foods are said to be expansive and acidic and include spices, sugars, soft drinks, and other stimulants. Yang foods include eggs, meats, and fish and are described as constrictive and alkaline. Both mental and physical problems are believed to follow from overconsumption of either yin or yang foods, which in turn creates an imbalance or disharmony in our bodies. Such an imbalance is analogous to the bipolar emotional disorder in which people cycle between depression and aggressive hyperactivity. The former condition follows from too much yin in one's diet, the latter from too much yang. But macrobiotic theory is also specific about the diverse health problems that can occur from failing to balance yin and yang foods. Too much in the way of yang foods, for example, is claimed to be associated with skin cancers, whereas eating excessive yin foods can lead to leukemia.

The rationales underlying these claims range from appeals to modern biochemistry to ancient Chinese medicine. More significant for this discussion is the assertion that our general worldview or spiritual orientation influences not only the foods we eat but also the way our bodies respond to and process these foods. Thus, someone with an extreme yang temperament (hypermasculine and aggressive) should not only try to balance this by consuming more yin foods but also try to cultivate a yin temperament. This can be accomplished through meditation and other yogic practices. And the food-temperament connection is said to work both ways, in that the foods we eat influence our temperament, whereas our temperament influences which foods we will *want* to eat. In short, macrobiotic theory argues that there is an intimate relationship between our food preferences and our mental or emotional status. Physical and mental-emotional health go together, and both depend on a harmonious balance of yin and yang tendencies.

Up to this point, discussion of the three food ideologies has generally been focused on how they can be understood as boundaries defining the everyday situations within which we negotiate our food behaviors. As individuals, we each develop idiosyncratic ways of dealing with the competing values that shape the ideologies of hedonism, nutritionism, and spiritualism. But over and above these intrinsic meanings associated with food, there is another, equally abstract, level at which food can be understood as an unmistakable embodiment of ideology. This occurs whenever specific foods serve, either by design or chance, as instruments or symbols of social or political ideologies.

During the Cold War between the Soviet Union and the U.S., for example, it was not unusual to see food described as an important instrument of foreign policy. The food aid provided by the U.S. to nonaligned countries—typically surplus wheat—was seen as a weapon in the contest between capitalism and Communism. And the ideological meaning embodied in this wheat was the superiority of the American capitalist system that produced it. Did the consumption of bread made from the U.S. wheat suddenly convince Third World peasants of the virtues of capitalism? Not likely. And, in fact, among the more aware leaders of some countries, it created resentment and anger at having to acknowledge food loans or charity, because such humanitarian aid often seemed to lead to increased U.S. military and commercial influence. After the arrival of famine relief, military missions, Coca-Cola, and infant formula would soon follow.

Quite apart from aid programs, American food products such as Coca-Cola and hamburgers have by now attracted consumers almost everywhere in the world. These food products have been criticized by many European and Third World intellectuals as subverting not only local cuisines but also the cultural traditions bound up in traditional food behaviors. What these critics perceive is not merely the invasion of alien fast foods and their negative impacts on local economies and traditions. As they see it, these foods carry an ideology of immediate sensual gratification and convenience that all too easily undermines traditional family values associated with social discipline and respect for authority. In effect, it is precisely those values impressed upon children and adolescents at the family table that are undermined by the ready availability of fast foods and other modern American convenience items. To put it more concretely, the child or teenager whose taste has been seduced by the sensual pleasure of hamburgers and colas may no longer look forward to a homemade meal, no longer value the effort that goes into its preparation, and no longer respect the traditional table manners and etiquette associated with eating it. This is the type of analysis and argument made by those who see in American fast foods the leading edge of cultural imperialism. Because where such foods first penetrate, other elements of the associated lifestyle are likely to follow. It is also the sort of analysis that allows foods to be perceived in terms of their symbolic, rather than their substantive, meaning, which in some situations can be directly relevant to ideological issues. When international political events create a surge of anti-American feelings in some parts of the world, for example, angry crowds will often throw stones at the local McDonald's franchise as well as at the U.S. embassy. And some intellectual critics of modernity have converted the McDonald's name into a pejorative verb, warning against the "McDonaldization" of their societies. In this usage, McDonaldization is the process whereby all or most other social values become subordinated to efficiency, convenience, and immediate gratification of artificial needs. All this, of course, follows from the entrepreneurial profit motive, and never mind the traditional values that get pushed to the wall.

The American counterargument to all this, and one that can occasionally be heard from a few foreign intellectuals as well, is that fast food brings a form of democratization to many parts of the world. By giving masses of people easy access to desirable items, it helps reduce some of the oppressive social class differences that traditional foods represent. It is noteworthy too that critics of the ideological values fast foods represent harbor deep resentment at the way their indigenous foods become transformed when they become popular in the U.S. If turnabout is fair play, then when a foreign food makes its way to the U.S. it ought to subvert or overwhelm some aspect of traditional American cuisine. But this doesn't seem to happen. For one thing, though some authorities disagree, most suggest that, because the U.S. is a nation of immigrants, it has little or nothing in the way of a traditional cuisine to be overwhelmed. Instead, as the food historian Raymond Sokolov has argued in *Fading Feast*, the U.S. has only an eclectic mixture of regional dishes that hardly meets the standard of a "cuisine." But, perhaps more to the point, when foreign foods enter the American mainstream, they are, much to the outrage of some critics, Americanized. The foods are usually modified to suit American tastes and mass production.

Pizza is probably the most outstanding example of this phenomenon. Over the past fifty years, it has certainly conquered America, yet it has done so only by becoming Americanized. Today's ubiquitous pizza franchises serve products that bear only a remote resemblance to the pizzas found in southern Italy or certain Italian restaurants in New York City fifty years ago. (Though I have heard it said that pizza was created in New Haven, Connecticut, and exported to Italy before returning to the U.S.) And when the traditional French breakfast croissant began to be marketed in American fast-food outlets and supermarkets, any visitor from France would have been disappointed in its flavor. Worse yet and adding insult to injury, in a typically American commercial move, the immigrant French croissant has been mated with the immigrant East European Jewish bagel to produce something called the "crobagel," and most Americans couldn't care less about its origins.

A similar fate has befallen Mexican tacos and burritos. The fast-food varieties are barely recognizable to Latino tastes, and the frozen supermarket varieties designed for microwaving depart even further from their ancestors. The McDonald's breakfast burrito provides yet another example of American culinary crossbreeding. Of all the foreign foods that have recently entered the U.S. mainstream, the one that has apparently come closest to retaining its integrity is salsa. This is probably because—apart from marketing it in mild, medium, and hot forms, and producing variations mixed with more vegetables or garlic—Americans have not found much of anything to do to salsa. It sells itself so well, in fact, that salsa has overtaken ketchup as the most popular condiment in America.

Taken together, the sociopolitical and cultural implications of food discussed in this chapter show that food can serve as a powerful container or carrier of ideology. It is not entirely absurd to suggest that the consumption of a given food is also, to some degree, the consumption of the moral or political values that item represents. And although the sociopolitical uses of food and the eating ideologies of hedonism, nutritionism, and spiritualism may appear far removed from one another, they connect very directly on the ground of pleasure. Coca-Cola has more or less conquered the world because it tastes good. That it may serve as an opening wedge for American cultural imperialism is quite secondary to its hedonic appeal. But in the image of young people in different parts of the world drinking Cokes while watching American films or TV programs, one can find at least strong symbolic support for seeing food as a carrier of hedonistic values. A poignant example of this has occurred during the ongoing conflict between Israelis and Palestinians. A colleague who recently returned from the area tells me that Palestinian children and teenagers who enjoyed eating pizza have given it up because it is viewed as a symbol of their enemy. And Palestinian restaurant owners are being discouraged from serving Israelis who enjoy Arab cuisine.

It may be useful, finally, to close the discussion of this whole topic by pointing out that one of the primary projects of the U.S. food industry today is to develop products that can close the gaps between the hedonistic, nutritional, and spiritual properties of food. Perhaps such an ideal can be realized with something like a delicious, no-fat, no-cholesterol pizza, super-fortified with vitamins and minerals and guaranteed to be neither too yin nor too yang, and kosher for Passover. Some aspects of this project are taken up later in chapter 8, which is devoted to the future of food. In the following chapter, however, we move backwards to a consideration of the past.

CHAPTER 5

From the Raw to the Cooked to the Haute Cuisine

T HE CONCLUDING LINE in *The Tractatus,* Ludwig Wittgenstein's classic discourse on the philosophy of science, asserts "Of that of which we cannot speak we must be silent." Scholars have generally taken this oracular statement to mean that some areas of human experience are simply not open to scientific investigation and had best be left alone. It bears directly on the topic at hand because a great eating experience, like great sex or other forms of visceral experience is, apart from saying that it was wonderful, also largely unspeakable. (And unless they are particularly gifted, those who insist on trying to speak of such matters invariably bore their listeners.) There are, of course, some important reasons for this situation, and, when it comes to food and cuisine, few scholars have attempted to go as deeply into them as Claude Lévi-Strauss and Sidney Mintz.

In *The Raw and the Cooked,* his masterwork on this subject, Lévi-Strauss analyzed the myths and folk traditions of primitive tribal groups, looking for explanations of how certain animal and vegetable substances in the natural environment were recognized as foods that eventually became the elements of cuisine. He found that the origins of the foods in common use could all be traced to mythic stories about the actions of some sort of godlike or quasi-human creature. The transformation of what is raw in nature to a food that can be cooked was, in other words, always attributed to a magical process personified and transmitted by a mythic, godlike figure. And then, of course, cooking itself requires a source of energy. Like other writers on the history of food, Lévi-Strauss suggests that this was initially the sun. Vegetables or animal parts exposed to dry in the sun become transformed from the raw, preserved from the decay that would otherwise quickly set in and prevent consumption. It is relevant that primitive myths invariably abound with sun gods, and it is only one more small step to the mythic origins of fire (with Prometheus as the major Western figure), fire still serving as the preeminent human instrument for transforming the raw to the cooked. It is fire that saves humans from the decay and putrefaction of their food when the sun disappears.

It is probably no mere coincidence that this analysis by Lévi-Strauss has its contemporary parallel in the status attributed to successful chefs and gastronomy authorities. They appear, after all, as Promethean masters of the culinary magic that can transform ordinary foodstuffs into taste delights. And most professional chefs are well aware of the hazards that go with their special status. As long as their magic works well, they are applauded, but if it fails or comes out badly, then like any godlike magician that disappoints, they may be cast aside. Those who deal in mystery and magic can never rest easy on their laurels. This may help explain why professional chefs are notoriously transient, always on the lookout for a new position.

But while the insights of Lévi-Strauss can illuminate some

of the problems of those who cook for a living, his general theory about the mythic origins of food and cuisine remains controversial. There is no such controversy, however, about the food theories developed by the distinguished anthropologist Sidney Mintz. His work has focused on the complex patterns of historical, economic, and biosocial factors underlying the development of specific foods and cuisines. The title of his 1996 book, *Tasting Food, Tasting Freedom: Excursions into Eating, Culture, and the Past*, clearly indicates his wide scope. Mintz describes the gradual dominance of sugar over honey as the preferred sweetener in most societies, referring to it as a "psychotechnical achievement"—psychological because of the conscious shift in taste preferences to the more readily available sugar, and technological because of the processing that sugar production requires. He also shows how Caribbean cuisine evolved from the conditions of plantation life imposed on African slaves and observes that the term "cuisine" is itself ambiguous. It derives from the Latin *coquere* (to cook) but is now used to designate the foods that are typically associated with particular nations or regions (even though, in our millennial global village, it is increasingly difficult to determine regional boundaries for any given cuisine). Mintz's eclectic studies of food suggest that, at best, the topic as a whole can be discussed only in loose generalizations. But if the focus is narrowed to specific foods, such as sugar, bread, corn, or potatoes, the uniqueness and complexity of the factors involved in the origins and developmental histories of these staples all but preclude anything except specialist research. There are whole volumes of research dedicated to each of these staples.

Any effort to speak seriously about cuisine, therefore, is

hemmed in on the one side by its origins in magic and mystery, and on the other side by the overwhelming complexity of its historical evolution. Nevertheless, there is now a rapidly expanding, diverse literature on food and cuisine, ranging from popular personal memoirs narrating the joys of eating in Portugal, Provence, Timbuktu, or wherever, to detailed scholarly monographs on cooking and cuisine in remote Spanish or Chinese villages. Falling in between is a seemingly endless river of social science studies on the eating habits of schoolchildren, teenagers, the elderly, males, females, Afro-Americans, and Hispanics. As the headline of a review in *Chronicle of Higher Education* put it, "More scholars focus on the historical, social and cultural meanings of food, but some critics say it's scholarship-lite." In fact, practically all this work deals with either narrow historical topics or the aesthetics and demographics of food and cuisine. There has been little or no effort to examine the deeper-lying psychological foundations of cuisine investigated by Lévi-Strauss and Mintz. This is the task addressed here, and it begins with a cautionary tale of how a plant failed to become a food accepted as part of a cuisine.

The plant is the Jerusalem artichoke. Not an artichoke at all but a variety of sunflower, it grows wild in much of North America. Its root forms a nutritious tuber that was once a staple item in the diet of Native Americans. It can also be used as animal feed or fermented to produce alcohol. But certain problems have blocked its development as a modern food crop. When consumed by humans, it causes a great deal of flatulence. Its small irregular shape makes it difficult to harvest by machine, and once harvested it rots quickly unless stored at special temperature and humidity conditions. But as described by my colleague Joseph Amato in *The Great Jerusalem Artichoke Circus*, the plant has enough virtues that, when the price of oil skyrocketed and the U.S. farm economy was severely depressed in the early 1980s, a few enthusiastic agribusiness entrepreneurs saw it as a new cash crop for farmers, and as a bonanza for those who could process it for alcohol on an industrial scale.

The leader of the business group was Fred Hendrickson, an attorney in Rapid City, North Dakota, who claimed that his inspiration to commercially exploit the Jerusalem artichoke occurred in 1980 when he observed several of these plants naturally thriving in an alley behind his home. Hendrickson read up on the plant and learned that it could be used to produce sugar, food products, and animal feed, as well as alcohol, which was already being widely used in Brazil as a fuel. Soon after, he experienced a quasi-religious vision of how the chokes could simultaneously revive the depressed farm economy and help resolve the U.S. energy crisis. It is also striking, with regard to Lévi-Strauss's metaphysical perspective on the origins of food, that Hendrickson was a born-again evangelical Christian who thought of the U.S. as the promised land and believed that he had a redemptive mission to help fulfill God's covenant with America.

Hendrickson began giving public talks about his vision. This led to an acquaintance with a well-off Minnesota businessman and fellow Christian, who offered to build a processing plant for extracting alcohol from the chokes. Their partnership was "blessed" by a local radio evangelist known as Pastor Pete who encouraged their sense of mission. In 1981, the two men formed American Energy Farming Systems. Pastor Pete's son was their first employee. The company then began a whirlwind marketing program, offering farmers, for $12,000, Jerusalem artichoke seed sufficient to plant ten acres. When the crop was harvested, it would supposedly be worth $40,000 per acre. Included in the deal were the company's promises to develop harvesting machinery and conduct the research needed to process the chokes into alcohol, sugar, livestock feed, and human food. Over the next eighteen months, enough farmers bought into this golden opportunity that, thanks to a quickly hired aggressive sales force made up of fundamentalist Christians selling seed contracts, the company took in approximately $26 million.

The Minnesota attorney general began investigating the company for fraud when it became clear that there was no real market for the crop, and that a small processing plant leased by the company was unable to extract much in the way of alcohol from the tubers. Additional complaints mounted, including misuse of funds by the company officers. In the spring of 1983, the company filed for bankruptcy. The partners were subsequently convicted of fraud; both served brief prison sentences, and the Jerusalem artichoke continues to grow wild.

This account of the failed Jerusalem artichoke project highlights the complex mix of social, psychological, and economic factors underlying efforts to convert something given in nature to a product that can be used for human consumption and fuel. Amato's narrative also provides a useful comparison with the development of soybeans, which required almost a hundred years of research and study before becoming a successful commercial product. A contemporary parallel can be seen in public anxiety about and resistance to irradiated vegetables, livestock growth hormones, and genetically altered plants. Some of this resistance is based on simple distrust of agribusiness corporations, but much of it runs deeper. Primordial, quasi-religious anxieties are triggered by the idea of men and women in white coats tampering with nature. European protesters chant "Franken (Frankenstein) foods" during their protest demonstrations and argue in other ways that appeal to the sacred status of food. Several years ago I gained a strong sense of their attitude, as well as European perspectives on the blend of historical, psychological, and aesthetic factors intrinsic to food, from observing the outdoor markets in Paris.

Once or twice a week in the residential neighborhoods of Paris, open-air markets are set up in the morning, flourish throughout the day, and then disappear by evening. Because of their sudden appearance and disappearance, and the extravagant cornucopia of foods displayed, the markets have an aura of magic. And there is also magic in the historical continuity they represent, for they have descended with little substantial change from the markets of the medieval walled town that became Paris, and from the Roman imperial culture of the time.

That these markets are still conducted in a communal style, with tables and stalls spread along the streets and sidewalks; that the meats, fishes, and cheeses sell nicely despite the presence of flies and the absence of any refrigeration except ice; and that the bloody hands of those selling meat emphasize the primal foundations of cuisine all combine to make the markets a powerful demonstration of both the historical and the social-psychological dimensions of food. And as the markets continually materialize on the pavements that cover the cobblestones that cover the cart tracks that were laid down along the trails of the Parissi Goths who first settled along the Seine River, they seem to preserve a uniquely human space defined by the forces of nature, culture, history, and technology. Consciously or not, the crowds of modern urban shoppers who enliven these markets participate in a profound gesture against the modern values of efficiency and convenience.

Erected in small city squares, on wide sidewalks near intersections, or on broad median strips, the displays of merchandise form either clusters or rows but are always facing each other across a shoppers' lane eight to ten feet wide. People carrying shopping bags or pulling two-wheeled carts along the lanes walk slowly, stopping now and then to buy something, to exchange greetings with other shoppers or vendors, or just to watch an activity that catches their eye. Knots of people sometimes block easy passage, but when this happens all present — those standing still and those wishing to pass — are able to sort themselves out according to an unstated, shared etiquette. The standees edge around to open a little way for people to get by, and the passersby in turn wait for this to happen before gently nudging their way through. Both groups maneuver their carts or bags with easy movements reflecting long practice. They never seem to get tangled up, and hardly a word is spoken aside from the occasional *"excusez."*

Even strangers fall into the pedestrian pattern without much difficulty. This may be because of the common sense dictated by the larger context: having entered the market, one can only merge with the currents of movement. In North American supermarkets, by contrast, the action is much faster paced and aggressive, if only because, apart from differences in national character, shoppers are free to move directly toward the items they want to buy and are more likely to have collisions or near misses with their large, four-wheeled shopping carts.

The obvious social discipline that prevails in the Paris markets seems a contradiction to North American common sense. Since the open-air markets are noisy from passing vehicles and the shouts of vendors, and there is really no firm separation from the larger street scene, and few if any police are present, the potential for confusion or conflict would seem much greater than in the enclosed North American supermarket. Yet the reality is just the reverse. Aside from the self-discipline of the shoppers, the explanation for this orderliness lies in the proprietary, supervisory presence of the vendors, who project an air of responsibility and control over their small territories. They radiate authority not only over their goods but also over the whole adjacent area. Their good-humored, commanding style appears to be a matter of tradition and personal pride, as well as commercial self-interest, since any serious disruption of the market's social dynamic would be bad for business. But it also contributes to the prevailing atmosphere of premodern social life, when personal relationships were an important part of most transactions.

This atmosphere is so strong that it makes the money transactions between vendors and their customers seem almost unimportant. As shoppers pause to examine items of interest, they are typically engaged in one or another sort of dialogue by the vendors. Thus bantering: "Madame, these apples from Normandy will not only help your digestion but improve your sex life!" Complimentary: "You have a good eye, *M'sieu*, these apples are the best of the season." Instructive: "You should try these apples baked for fifteen minutes with cinnamon and nutmeg." Customers, for their part, may challenge the vendor on the price or quality of an item, or ask why something they want is not available. Often too, anyone stopping to look at a display of cheese or fruit will be offered a sample. Once a purchase is made, the social process usually continues, so that, while wrapping a purchase or making change, vendors may suggest other things that would go well with the item in hand, or point out what a good buy the customer has made.

There is also a good deal of personal conversation. Vendors and their customers sometimes have known each other for years and will inquire about the health of their families and their children's progress in school, or make comments about the weather. If a conversation should develop about cooking or the quality of goods for sale, it is not unusual for passersby to join in. A vendor might even appeal to a passing shopper to verify the taste or quality of an item. Much of this interplay is accompanied by lively jokes or gestures, and political references are often made to the effect that only a communist or conservative or what-have-you would do or say or eat this or that.

Contrary to our stereotypes, one thing that never seems to occur is serious bargaining. A vendor might throw in something extra with a purchase or, especially toward the end of the day, offer to sell some items at a reduced price, but haggling over prices is rare. This is not to say that customers never complain that the price of a fish or cabbage is *trop cher*—too dear. But if they do, the response is usually a joke about government economic policies or that the price is high because it is the end of the season for the item. A vendor may also suggest that the customer buy a similar but less expensive item.

Many of these interchanges show that the vendors either know their customers quite well or can shrewdly size them up. Occasionally they will call out to shoppers at a distance to let them know that a particular item is available or has been put aside specially for them. And shoppers frequently demonstrate more than a casual knowledge about the items for sale. This shows up in the apparent expertise of their browsing as well as their comments and questions. It is not unusual to see one shopper give an unsolicited recommendation of an item to another, or warn against its purchase. There is, then, a feeling of professionalism about both the shopping and the selling. In any case, the sheer plethora of foods on display requires significant shopping expertise.

Part of the attraction of the market is surely the profusion of its foods. This is powerfully enhanced by its immediacy: the abundance and diversity of foods are felt directly, at the most primitive sensory level. Unavoidable and unmediated by air conditioning, the smells, sounds, and sights of foods in the raw create a physical relationship with the world of organic nature that in North America is usually masked by enclosed display cases and slick packaging. This primordial quality of the market is so intimately linked with the social processes involved—one inhales its substance even as one immerses in the milieu— that any further analysis of the total market experience would be meaningless. The totality is simply greater than the sum of its parts.

Why should this experience of the market be so attractive to crowds of people with varying tastes, traditions, and ethnic backgrounds? Although almost any theory of social behavior can provide plausible answers, I am inclined toward the ideas of Carl Jung, Sigmund Freud, and Claude Lévi-Strauss. Jungian theory would suggest that the market evokes a deep-lying response from the collective unconscious, wherein food is inextricably bound up in the feelings of security provided by tribal social life. Freudian theory would appeal to the pleasurable id impulses stimulated by the market and its general atmosphere of spontaneous sensuality reminiscent of childhood. And followers of Lévi-Strauss might interpret the attractiveness of the market in terms of its mythic significance: its primitive but essential function as mediator between the raw and the cooked. This view also suggests that the open-air markets are so appealing because they bring a tangible touch of the wild into the midst of urban modernity. Perhaps as nothing more than an unconscious affirmation of our solidarity with nature, the whole of rationalized industrial culture may here be shrugged off in that existential moment when the fish for dinner is wrapped in yesterday's *Le Monde* newspaper.

Whether it occurs in one of the Paris markets or in a mom-and-pop grocery in Brooklyn, when we go shopping for the foods that fit our particular notions of cuisine, we are essentially foraging. This is a behavior that can be traced as far back as our remote human ancestors, as well as to the monkeys and chimps that are our close relatives. But since most of us have practiced our foraging instinct only in shops and markets, we are not well prepared for survival in the wild. This is why one of the principles taught in jungle-survival schools is to emulate the foraging of chimps and monkeys: whatever they eat will usually be safe for us. And, of course, we can also eat the chimps and monkeys. More to the point, however, is that, just as the foraging behaviors of apes are essentially social activities, in the sense of being a collective group process, so it is with most of us today: we mainly seek out and consume only those things identified by our group or society as being good to eat. Just reflect for a moment: does any of us ever try a novel food that has not been directly or indirectly recommended by someone we trust?

The psychological foundations of cuisine apparently rest on the foraging that acquires the raw food our group (and this can include friends, family, or the food editor of the *New York Times*) identifies as desirable. The various cuisines already begin to take on their basic structure at this point because the availability and desirability of foods vary between groups. This seems simple enough except that an immediate paradox presents itself. The moment we enter the domain of cuisine, it is not merely the acquired raw items that determine what will be cooked. Equally or more significantly, it is the result of the cooking that determines the raw items to be acquired. That is, raw items are not in themselves desirable. It is what these items can become once they have been processed and then transformed by the technology we call cooking that is desirable. This means that, in certain respects, cuisine—the image of a finished product, as it were—can influence or dominate the shopper-forager's perception of the raw food items. To see a dead chicken is to already see its potential as the main course of Sunday's dinner. And to select one of several dead chickens is to superimpose the image of a future event on the present moment of selection.

For most of us in modern societies, the cognitive leap from raw to cooked is shortened by commercial processing. Instead of a chicken carcass complete with head, feet, and feathers, what we see in the supermarket is a clean, neatly packaged, and perhaps frozen object that has already come more than halfway the distance from being a dead chicken to a Sunday dinner. But whether chicken, fish, beef, or vegetable, *denaturalization* is the first important step toward the item's transformation to cuisine. This is the critical issue in the understanding of cuisine. To denaturalize an object is to separate it from its place in the order of nature. The apples on display in the market are no more the same as they were when hanging from the tree branch than the chickens in the market are the same as they were at the poultry farm. Both have been removed from their original contexts and processed out of their natural states. The apples have been picked, washed, sorted, and crated; the chickens have been put through more elaborate preparation procedures, including, among Orthodox Jews, the slaughtering ritual that certifies them as kosher, and purified for human consumption. In general, the higher we look on the food chain, the more elaborate are the denaturalizing procedures. Much of this, of course, appears to be no more than common sense, a matter of public health and sanitation, let alone consumer convenience. But there are also a number of psychological benefits of denaturalization.

Foremost among these is the relief from guilt. The higher we go up the food chain, the closer we come to ourselves, and the greater becomes the need for some sort of procedure to alleviate potential guilt feelings associated with killing and cannibalism. There is, first of all, the biblical commandment "Thou shalt not kill." Granted, this doesn't trouble most of us—some Buddhists excepted—when it comes to vegetables. But it shows up strongly in connection with mammals. If this seems implausible, consider the evidence from cattle slaughterhouses, where there is always a high turnover of the workers who do the killing. Even though they are well paid, they find the work emotionally debilitating. There is also the testimony of hunters, who occasionally report hesitating or failing to shoot an animal because of its natural beauty. In his memoir *The Green Hills of Africa*, Ernest Hemingway felt it necessary to justify his killing of big game animals by saying that he felt no guilt so long as he killed "cleanly" and saw to it that the meat and hides did not go to waste. But in another passage he mentions that once, when in great pain from a gunshot wound, he thought, "Perhaps what I was going through was a punishment for all hunters."

In any case, virtually all primitive human groups developed rituals to be followed after the killing of any animal. The larger and more important the animal was as a source of food, the more complex the ritual. Native Americans in the western U.S., for example, not only relied on the buffalo for food and clothing but also identified with it to some extent and saw it as the generous provider of essentials for survival. By carrying out rituals expressing gratitude and requesting forgiveness, they could diminish the guilt associated with the killing of this important provider. The subsequent cutting and sharing of the carcass further denaturalizes the animal. It allows dead buffalo to become meat for cooking, which, when cooked, becomes stew for eating. Through this sequence, most of the guilt is dissipated. If, in our modern situation, any vestiges of guilt remain, a brief ritual blessing or prayer can always be pronounced before digging in to the meal.

Rituals are generally understood to be psychological mechanisms for dealing with tension and anxiety. They can take many forms. The origins of cuisine lie first of all in the ritualized guidelines developed in different cultures specifying which vegetable and animal matter should or should not be considered food. They become integrated into group traditions because, by renouncing certain items, the anxiety or guilt arising from eating others is relieved. At the same time, group cohesion and solidarity are enhanced. By following the rules defining kosher foods, for example, Jews can not only reduce their guilt feelings about consuming certain God-given life forms, but may also feel superior to those who do not follow these laws. Among Catholics, the former tradition of not eating meat on Friday had a similar function. Cuisine, then, has its beginnings in the range of items approved by the culture or group as edible.

Ritualized procedures extend to the harvesting of crops, since we experience some degree of anxiety whenever we tamper with any of the natural or God-given life forms, including plants. And so, denaturalization takes place all along the line, from the field or forest to the items that finally come off the cooking fire or out of the modern kitchen. Every culture specifies traditional ways for meats, fish, and vegetables to be cleaned and readied for cooking, and proper preparation by the cook or food handlers is an important part of this. In many societies, cooking was a spiritually significant activity reserved for those individuals—priests, shamans, and their retainers—thought to be in close touch with the forces of nature. This tradition persists in various ways. The good Buddhist or Brahmin may recite a mantra or offer incense to purify himself or herself before beginning to cook. And in many cultures, the attitudes or emotions of the cook are thought to influence the outcome of his or her effort. There is an appealing functional quality to such traditions: by saying a prayer or taking time to focus ourselves on the task before us, we are less likely to make mistakes in our cooking. Ritual validates itself by acting as a practical remedy for the tensions or anxieties that frequently accompany cooking. Whoever cooks, after all, can hardly avoid some degree of anxiety, since he or she is likely to be judged by the outcome of the work. Many people avoid cooking for precisely this reason. In contrast, others devote a great deal of effort to it, in an attempt to gain social approval and a sense of personal achievement or even social power. Although there may be some societies in which good cooks are not appreciated, in most human groups they have a privileged position. And are there not countless tales and stories of cooks who carefully prepare a meal designed to represent their feelings of love, or sometimes contempt, for those who will eat it?

In addition to the various rules of edibility that have governed the evolution of cuisines, including the availability of spices and condiments, cooking technologies have played a critical role. These technologies include both the forms of energy employed—from the sun and the open fire to the microwave oven—and the tools or instruments, ranging from green wood sticks to Teflon pans and food processors. Where I grew up in New York City in the 1940s, boys of ten or twelve years occasionally reproduced what must be one of the most primitive of all cooking technologies. We roasted potatoes (preferably stolen), called "mickeys," in fires we made in empty lots using broken-up orange crates. We left our mickeys in the fire until the skins were coal black and then ate them, spiced only with the smoke. It dawned on me many years later that potatoes cooked in this fashion were probably called mickeys because of their association with Irish immigrants. Having subsequently inhaled a good deal of smoke while cooking over open fires in the Boy Scouts, on camping trips, and in the army (though, in the latter case, a C-ration can partly filled with dirt soaked with a judicious amount of gasoline was preferred to open fires), I am convinced that avoiding smoke was a major motivating factor in the development of cooking stoves.

Archeological evidence indicates that roasting and baking are the earliest forms of cooking, most likely discovered by Paleolithic groups when food was accidentally dropped in a fire or placed on a stone next to it. The forerunner of our modern rotisserie, whereby meat is cooked on a spit made of green wood or an animal bone, soon followed. No clear evidence exists to explain the discovery of boiling, but one interesting hypothesis is that it may have evolved from attempts to roast an intact animal stomach on a spit. Since the contents of the stomach would include some liquid as well as partially digested solid matter, the latter would get boiled. And since the solid matter might well be a mixture of flesh, grasses, and roots, this might also explain how it was discovered that the flavor of animal flesh could be enhanced by herbal material, the precursor of spices. The Scottish haggis could well be an artifact of this stomach-cooking procedure. Aside from spits and stomachs, the earliest utensils included concave stones, turtle shells, and other objects that could hold water for boiling. When placed over heat in a turtle shell or clamshell with little or no water, animal parts containing fat would have sizzled sufficiently to alert our Paleolithic ancestors to the possibilities of frying. According to Reay Tannahill's 1973 summary of archeological evidence, by the beginning of the neolithic period, around 10,000 B.C., the basic ways of cooking had already developed among groups of hunter-gatherers and only remained to be adapted to the grain products that emerged among the early agricultural groups.

These cooking technologies, particularly the instruments and utensils employed, have evolved from their primitive origins to the extraordinarily complex array of implements available today. Indeed, without expert guidance, many of the items on display at any good kitchenware shop or department store defy understanding of their functions. But the basic ways of cooking, except for microwaving, are relatively unchanged. A noteworthy social class interpretation of cooking methods was suggested by Lévi-Strauss, who thought roasting was an upperclass or aristocratic method because it involved a considerable shrinkage of meats, which only the well-off could afford. Boiling, on the other hand, saves everything in the pot, including the liquified nutrients, and so was preferred by the poor.

This distinction certainly fits the historical and archeological evidence. Throughout the centuries ranging from the Middle Ages to the end of the Victorian era, the only major cooking implements owned by poor peasants and workers were a good-sized pot or cauldron and a few pans. Meals for the most part consisted of whatever edibles were available for boiling in cauldrons hung in fireplaces. Some of my own childhood experience confirms this: high cuisine for my East European immigrant parents often consisted of nothing more than a boiled chicken, with feet, neck, and liver included.

The various cuisines that exist today and can in some respects be traced back to our hunter-gatherer ancestors are all products of the different ways locally available foods became combined with cooking technologies and cultural values specifying edibility. Clearly, it's impossible to even briefly summarize the unique evolution of various cuisines without writing another book. But we can still appreciate the psychological mechanisms involved, because they relate to how people generally adapted to a handful of limiting conditions. First among these conditions is nature: the climatic and other environmental factors dictating what kinds of foods were consistently available in the various regions. Olive oil, for example, was plentiful in southern Europe and became a central component of Italian and Greek cuisine. Throughout northern Europe, with its greater concentration of livestock, animal fats were a central component. It is no exaggeration to say that, up until the 18th century, cuisine in northern and eastern Europe was largely determined by struggles for survival in the face of nature and social instability. The shortages and famines caused by crop failures, warfare, and banditry—the same conditions that exist in parts of Africa today—meant that people had to make do with whatever edibles came to hand. But these conditions of instability also encouraged celebrations and feast days. The threat of theft by roving bandits and confiscation by mercenary soldiers, not to mention rot, meant that storing food stocks was not practical. Orgiastic feasting when food was plentiful, as at harvest times, was an adaptive response to the problem of what to do with surplus.

By the beginning of the 18th century, several new conditions paved the way for more elaborate regional cuisines. Improved food-storage techniques, increased public order, and social stability associated with the growing power of nation-states all led to change. These conditions allowed food to become more than a matter of survival for the masses, and more than an extravagant show of plenty for the aristocracy. Banqueting had earlier been chiefly an occasion to display near-random quantities of foodstuffs, often arranged in eccentric combinations designed to impress guests with the power of the host. This pattern now shifted toward a greater concern with quality and aesthetics, as the criteria of high social status came to include refined tastes and elaborate table manners. A rise in literacy at this time allowed recipes and dining arrangements to be more freely exchanged, and expanded opportunities for trade and travel encouraged a wider range of comparisons to be made between them.

In *The History of Manners*, Norbert Elias refers to this change in the meaning of food as being bound up in the general "civilizing" trend that took root in Europe toward the end of the Middle Ages but which began to influence large numbers of people only during the 18th century. One significant aspect of the civilizing trend was the appearance of the first restaurants in Paris during the latter part of that century. Up to that time, hungry travelers had to take whatever they could get at the single common table found in public lodging houses or inns. Restaurants began as small shops or stands specializing in soups called *"restaurants"* (restoratives), served to passersby needing a refreshing snack. These shops evolved into places where people could sit at private tables and order from a menu.

According to Elias, the refinements of daily-life behavior, including ways of cooking and eating, that first took hold among the upper classes were gradually adopted by the growing middle class. It then became an important mechanism of social mobility for those who aspired to higher social status, a point that appears repeatedly in 18th- and 19th-century novels. More specifically, Elias sees the increased prevalence of public stability and security as being what in large part allowed greater numbers of people to acquire a stronger sense of self-determination and personal discipline—what we today call cognitive control—over their eating habits.

It was also in the 18th century that systematic discussions of manners and cooking first became widely available to the emerging middle class. French philosopher Denis Diderot's influential mid-century *Encyclopédie* contained a substantial article on cuisine. It described recipes and food practices throughout much of the civilized world, and the effects of diet on health. The *Encyclopédie* article makes it clear that by this time, at least among the literate segments of the population, many of what we consider to be the modern factors influencing our views of cuisine were already in place. And various sections of the article are directly in line with contemporary views. There are warnings against excessive use of seasonings and sauces, as this can cause health problems, and because cooks may use condiments to cover up poor-quality foods. Religious and moral issues are discussed in terms of the lust or sensuality that can be stimulated by overindulging in rich foods, while "corruption" of the sense of taste is seen as both a moral and a physiological hazard. These perspectives were echoed by some physicians and other prominent writers of the period, such as Jean-Jacques Rousseau. All emphasized the virtues of a plain diet. In general, however, the cuisine and food habits of the masses remained relatively primitive during the 18th century.

It was only in the 19th century that all the social, cultural, and scientific underpinnings of modern Western cuisines came into play. Modes of food preservation, storage, and transportation radically improved during the industrial revolution, bringing greater quantities of better-quality foods within reach of ordinary people, many of whom could now for the first time attempt to practice healthier food habits. And a new trend in the social and emotional meanings of food began among the upper classes and trickled down to the rest of society. First promoted in France, most notably through the gastronomic writings of Anthelme Brillat-Savarin, who is credited with inspiring a new set of aesthetic standards for food behaviors, this trend inverted conceptions of eating. Instead of a meal being carefully prepared simply to enhance the celebration of a special occasion, the meal itself was now the occasion for celebration. And, for the first time, it became fashionable to believe that the character and sensibilities of individuals were revealed by their eating habits. This was not just a question of table manners; it extended to the person's ability to appreciate, conceptualize, and converse intelligently about the quality of various cuisine items. Former U.S. president Thomas Jefferson was well known for his ability to do this. He was a fully realized prototype for the 19th-century "gentleman of quality" who could identify vintage wines, discuss the ingredients of dishes being served, hold forth on various recipes, and even expand on the historical events associated with their origins. Many of these abilities have been packaged and epitomized for today's movie audiences in the character of James Bond.

Over and above the manners and pretensions, the substance itself of high cuisine began to reach the masses. This occurred both symbolically, via cookbooks and gossip from the legions of servants employed by the wealthy, and concretely — at least in Paris — through the odd, mostly clandestine, trade in leftovers.

As described by French historian Jean-Paul Aron, "the art of using leftovers" was widely practiced in Paris during the latter part of the 19th century. Leftovers would be sold to middlemen at the back doors of the grand hotels and homes of the rich, reappear in popular restaurants, and the remnants often sold again to working-class Parisians. The quality of the leftovers depended on their age. As noted by one 19th-century observer, they were "tasty the first day, acceptable the second, languishing the third, and after that increasingly nasty!" Apart from its utility as a questionable form of recycling, the practice carried substantial significance for French cuisine because it prompted innovative uses of sauces that could revive and refurbish second- or third-hand items. On the other hand, it also caused enough illnesses and deaths that the Parisian authorities imposed an inspection program designed to wipe out the trade.

During the same period, a wide variety of cookbooks aimed at the middle- and working-class masses were being published. They sold so well that cookbooks soon became a major source of profit for authors and publishers, establishing a tradition of consistently high sales that persists today. But the rapid proliferation of mass-marketed cookbooks—which increasingly included not only recipes but also instructions on household management, table manners, and the moral responsibilities of housewives for maintaining the health of their families—also marked another important change in the meaning of cuisine. Cuisine now began to realize its modern function as a vehicle of cultural and social values. To some extent, this had always been true, but from about the 1860s onward, this function was no longer limited to the upper echelons of society. Insofar as the conceits of the elites were embodied in their food habits, these were being revealed in cookbooks—Queen Victoria's chief cook published one in 1845—and eagerly assimilated by the growing middle classes.

The popular cookbooks also began to reflect distinctive approaches to food preparation. A prime example appeared in the best-selling Fanny Farmer book. First published in 1896 as *The Boston Cooking-School Cook Book*, it would become widely known by the name of its author, who was director of the school. What set this work apart was its focus on the precise measurement of recipe ingredients. Instead of referring to the traditional pinch of salt, dash of pepper, or chunk of butter, as previous cookbook authors did, Farmer specified exact quantities in a way that seemed a clear counterpart to the norms of efficiency emerging in American industrial society. The psychological effect was to reduce the uncertainties that invariably plague novices in the kitchen. And in many ways, this innovation can be seen as a move that began reducing the art of cooking to a technology, one that would reach its peak in the standardization and efficiency now on display at McDonald's, Pizza Hut, and other fast-food outlets.

The popularization of cuisine also began to show up toward the end of the 19th century in the brief food sections of newspapers and the more elaborate articles on cooking and dining in women's magazines. Although initially focused on recipes and often related to the products advertised in the publication, these food advisories and recommendations became the spawning ground for a new species that would emerge full-blown during the first half of the 20th century: the food maven, an all-round celebrity-expert on cooking, cuisine, dining in, and dining out.

Betty Crocker is the exemplary case of a popular expert who dispensed advice aimed at working- and middle-class housewives. She was created by Marjorie Husted, who worked in the advertising department of General Mills in the 1920s. Part of Husted's job was to answer letters of inquiry from consumers. She needed a catchy signature, and her boss suggested "Crocker" as the surname, because it belonged to a popular former company director. Her colleagues agreed that "Betty" would make a popular first name. Husted became so good at the letter writing that it grew into a newspaper advice column. She presented herself as a cheerful, friendly authority who sympathized with the problems of young married women worried about providing their husbands with attractive but nutritious meals. Her Betty Crocker advice column quickly attracted a large readership and was syndicated. Later on, in 1927, she reached an even larger audience with an NBC radio program called *The Betty Crocker Cooking School of the Air*. Her remarkable popularity was confirmed in 1945 when a survey reported that she was the best-known woman in the U.S. after Eleanor Roosevelt and was referred to as "the First Lady of food." In 1947, General Mills attached the name Betty Crocker to a cake-mix product. This proved so successful that it is now the brand name for approximately twenty-four items, ranging from hamburger helper to instant mashed potatoes.

One reason for Husted's success had no direct connection with her intrinsic appeal to housewives. Instead, it had to do with the rapid growth of public interest in the new findings of nutrition science. This material was and still is being spread far and wide by home economists and dieticians. On the one hand, it had the effect of making traditional forms of cooking and cuisine appear unhealthy or obsolete. On the other hand, it was often too scientistic for busy homemakers looking for easily understandable ways to prepare certifiably tasty, healthy meals. Betty Crocker, and her imitators at popular women's magazines, offered this guidance, and put an appealing human face on it. Fundamentally, however, their success was probably because they provided anxious young women with a kind of culinary therapy, relieving their anxiety about all the myriad food choices and nutrition principles generated by modern science.

The typical housewives of the 1920s, '30s, and '40s could rely on their Betty Crockers and were not concerned with gourmet specialties—there were no electric mixers or food processors in those days. But as our society became more affluent, another, more contemporary and rather intellectual, brand of advice on cooking and cuisine was developed by writers such as Julia Child, Craig Claibourne, and M.F.K. Fisher. Their work created a new philosophy of cuisine that went against the prevalent view of cooking as a boring chore. Blending esoteric recipes with personal anecdotes and sophisticated kitchen chit-chat that focused on the joys of gourmet cooking and eating, they persuaded many people to take gourmet cuisine seriously, and to view labor-intensive cooking as a desirable hobby.

The gourmet-cookbook philosophers appealed as much to men as they did to women, particularly to well-off divorced or bachelor males aspiring to the glamorous lifestyle of James Bond or Hugh Heffner. *Playboy* magazine even ran articles advising readers how to prepare sexually seductive meals. And the line of descent from Fanny Farmer through Betty Crocker and Julia Child has now apparently culminated in a baker's dozen of celebrity chefs with attractive TV personalities and cuisine-appropriate foreign accents. Their appeal seems based on the superficial intimacy provided by all successful performers on weather, sports, and talk shows. Indeed, many of these celebrity chefs made their TV debuts as talk-show guests who could offer viewers an "up close and personal" experience of cooking, while chatting up the audience with a flow of good-humored comments.

If TV celebrity chefs are one of the newest variations on the theme of food and cuisine as entertainment, one of the oldest is the breed of food mavens known as restaurant critics. Like literary, art, and music critics, restaurant critics have a history as long as their subject matter, and they provide a similar function, namely to explain and communicate the fine points and esoterica of their subject matter to ordinary folks. Moreover, and again like other critics, influential restaurant critics have the ability to make or break the enterprises they evaluate. What appears to be most significant about these critics, at least those such as Mimi Sheraton in New York or La Reynière in Paris, who attained celebrity status is their single-minded focus on aesthetics. Central, of course, is the sensory aesthetic: the taste qualities of food.

Describing the tastes of various food items in specific detail is a difficult task, lying well beyond the abilities of most of us. It demands the ability to translate sensory experiences and feelings about those experiences into language that will convey immediate visceral meanings to a reader or listener. This requires expert application of a specialized vocabulary and stock of metaphors to the food experiences in question. Mimi Sheraton raised this skill to high art while writing a restaurant column for the *New York Times* in the 1980s. Thus, she might describe the general quality of a given dish in positive terms such as "authoritative," "interesting," "cooly light," "classic," "sparkling," or just plain "delicious." Lesser items might be noted as "perfunctory," "undistinguished," "innocuous," "bland," or "marred." The really disliked items would be put down as "tasteless," "characterless," "overpowering," or "mushy." Particular flavors and other specific food qualities were described with terms such as "starchy," "sunny," "stinging," "earthy," "acidic," "rich," "bright," and "soggy."

Sheraton's ability to deploy this sort of vocabulary in an interesting way while also commenting on the restaurant's service, decor, and atmosphere became something of a model for other North American food and restaurant commentators. She took a direct, empirical approach to food that closely approximated the practical, empirical values of North American society. This stands in sharp contrast to the writings of influential French critics, who frequently employ a language of food emphasizing historical, regional, and personal references. Thus, when they approve of a dish, they tend to say things like "To taste the bouillabaisse offered by Chef Alphonse is to taste the very heart of Mediterranean cuisine" or "The hearty pea soup recalled the same feelings of satisfaction we felt as schoolboys on chilly winter evenings." Disapproval, on the other hand, might bring on remarks like "This meager repast was enough to dishonor five hundred years of Norman tradition" or "Anyone who values his liver would do well to avoid the quiche."

The language employed to communicate experiences with food is, at least among the professionals, quite specialized. It is also anchored in the cultural values held by people in different societies and social classes, who frequently eat different cuisines. I have yet to discover, though they may well be out there, critics with a language appropriate for comparing the virtues of a McDonald's Big Mac with those of a Burger King Whopper, or a Domino's pizza with the Godfather's. Yet if there is no Mimi Sheraton of fast food, one might easily be invented. This is because all foods, regardless of their cultural or social class associations, are susceptible to critical evaluation and discussion.

The successful food critics can be taken as the exception proving the rule that it is difficult to speak of visceral experiences such as eating in a meaningful way. Although this chapter has focused on the development of Western European and North American cuisines, the social and psychological processes involved appear to be quite general. That is, the mechanisms by which most of the raw animal, vegetable, and mineral material available to human beings first becomes defined as food, and second as cuisine, are apparently universal. And if there is any one conclusion to be drawn from the various perspectives discussed, it is this: throughout most of human history, the meanings associated with food have steadily evolved along with the social and technological changes that have increased its availability and our ways of consuming it.

CHAPTER 6

Champagne Slippers, the Twinkie
Defense, and He-Man Diets

S CIENCE FICTION WRITERS and "futurists" in the 1930s,
'40s, and '50s were fond of suggesting that, by the 21st
century, when all the basic nutrients could be easily synthesized in sufficient quantities, food as we have known it would
disappear and be replaced by pills containing everything necessary for a perfectly balanced diet. Like some of the other
popular predictions in that era of high scientism—by now we
are all supposed to be commuting to work in our autogiros or
Buck Rogers flying belts—they were wrong. But not entirely.
Consider that today in every supermarket a wide range of vitamins, minerals, energy bars, and other nutritional supplements
is available, and that almost every shopping mall has its health-
food store with an even wider selection of supplements. For
the most part, however, people are no more inclined to give up
the pleasures of the table in favor of synthesized nutrients than
they are to give up sexual intercourse in favor of pornography
and artificial insemination. The real things are too attractive,
and we are driven toward both by the most powerful of our
human appetites.

In the next chapter, there will be more to say about the
future of food, including the psychological factors that make

predicting future trends in what we eat and the way we eat very chancy. The more immediate issues considered here are the various ways food relates to the two most powerful and fundamental of human drives or appetites: sex and aggression. And because consideration of aggression leads quite naturally to the role of food in the military, where it takes on some particular social and emotional meanings, this topic will also be discussed. In certain respects, military uses of food have always reflected the conventional eating patterns of the larger society, but contemporary trends in the development of military rations may influence future changes in civilian foods.

In addition to sex and aggression, there are many other significant human motives relevant to food. But according to Sigmund Freud, who should never be underrated when it comes to the visceral human appetites, most of them grow out of basic sexual and aggressive instincts. And these deserve particular attention for two reasons: first, because they are necessary for survival, tied to the nurturing that newborns require if they are to thrive; second, because in one form or another, they are with us for the rest of our lives.

What is initially most obvious about the relationship between food and sex, though rarely remarked on except by Freudians, is that apart from food and drink, and the incidental oral pacifiers such as cigarettes, cigars, pipes, and chewing gum, the only other things we willingly take in our mouths are the preferred body parts of our sex partners. As first theorized by Freud, the infant sucking at the breast is experiencing the original source, and subsequent basis, for all sensual pleasure. The skin-to-skin body contacts and baby talk during nursing are virtually inseparable from the pleasure of feeding and as such are thought to be the foundation for all later erotic experiences. It should not be surprising, then, that for the rest of our lives there is at least an implicit if not explicit link between food and sex. Indeed, there are terms commonly associated with pleasurable sexual experiences, such as "orgy" or "orgiastic," that are also commonly applied to pleasurable eating experiences. And in France, great sex and great food are both said to produce the feeling of *jouissance*, which roughly translates as intense visceral satisfaction.

More specifically, partners in the act of passionate sex are in a near-literal sense consuming each other. This could be why we refer to newlyweds as "consummating" their marriage. But before any such ultimate consummation, for most couples there is usually a less dramatic phase of acquaintance that almost always involves the sharing of food. In North American culture, the dinner date is the time-honored first step toward intimacy. If this goes well, the next move is often a home-cooked meal prepared by one member of the couple. No matter what the sequence, generally some sort of progression toward sexual intimacy occurs through the medium of shared food consumption. Marriage itself is universally celebrated with feasting on foods that convey the status, values, and ethnicity of the couple, or at least of the family responsible for organizing the wedding. Pretensions to respectable social status, not to mention materialistic values, are typically signified by lavish quantities of expensive delicacies and drinks. If the bride and groom are from different ethnic groups, there will likely be an appropriate mix of ethnic cuisines, and if they are devoted vegetarians, the wedding feast may also reflect this value.

Once the ceremonial dust and honeymoon excitement

settle, the food and sexual activities of the couple inevitably face the challenge of making the transition from novelty items to elements of daily-life routine. Initially, no matter how similar their food preferences may have appeared to be before marriage or cohabitation, some degree of compromise is necessary. All the almost-infinite variety of food details that are rarely noted or else ignored as trivial during courtship can become problematic. What brand of mustard or ketchup is preferred? Should the breakfast cereal be with or without raisins? Are the peanuts and potato chips to be salted, lightly salted, or unsalted? Name brand or generic? Frozen juices, bottled, or fresh? One or another cut of meat?

All these uncertainties typically get ironed out during the first few years and become routine. And the same descent into routine often applies to sex. After a few years, desire may become less imperative: seductive foreplay is reduced or eliminated, body odors and gestures once ignored become irritating, and romance declines as the prosaic effects of illness, snoring, and unpleasant toilet habits are encountered. (Was ever a young woman entirely happy with her man's toilet habits? Or young man pleased to find his woman's stockings hanging in the shower stall?) In the long run, both food and sex may reach the point at which couples begin to lose their appetites. Monotony takes its toll, whether it is from the same old chicken every Sunday dinner or the missionary position every Saturday night. Then, too, appetites may change direction as people mature. Clearly, despite the absence of stimulating cuisine and sex, marriages can be sustained for many years by other factors, but if both food and sex become a burdensome source of dissatisfaction, then, as marriage counselors can testify, the relationship is likely to fail.

There is some surprising evidence of a symmetry between the role of food in the development of intimacy during courtship and in the failure or rejection of intimacy that can precede divorce. According to an unusual study conducted in England, married couples frequently reach the point of splitting up during arguments at the dinner table. It is certainly arguable that the last straw has been reached when a marriage decays to the level of bitter recriminations while sharing food. And although I have not found any systematic studies showing that the food habits of people change after they separate or divorce, this too seems to be quite common. When couples split up, whatever compromises they may have made over their personal food preferences may now be reversed, and whatever foods stand out as special favorites of their former mate may now be avoided because of their painful associations. Despite the sexist implications, common experience also suggests that, following divorce, women usually begin dieting to lose weight, whereas their former spouses regress to a convenience cuisine composed of fast foods, TV dinners, and take-out items.

A very different kind of anecdotal evidence emphasizing the intermingling of food and sex can be found in accounts of esoteric sexual behaviors. Although cases in which one or both sex partners are said to cover parts of their bodies with honey, whipped cream, strawberry jam, or other tasty foods (it never seems to be oatmeal or mashed potatoes) may be more prevalent as fantasy than reality, the idea of enjoying two fundamental sensual pleasures simultaneously is a favorite in erotic literature. Less extreme but carrying similar connotations is the gesture by 19th-century playboys, who supposedly demonstrated their devotion by drinking champagne out of their girlfriends' slippers.

A more direct link between food and sex is in the imagery frequently associated with sex organs. It is based mainly on appearances. For example, the banana is the ubiquitous surrogate for a penis, but a zucchini, corncob, or almost any phallic-looking sausage can also serve. Following the same principle, representations of female breasts are usually melons, grapefruits, or coconuts, whereas the vagina may be equated to an oyster, sometimes an artichoke, or a pitted half peach. While all these food surrogates are relatively benign, the dream symbols of sex organs celebrated in Freudian theory are invariably threatening: snakes and elephant trunks for the penis; open manholes, sewers, and wells for the vagina. The distinction seems to depend on the presence or absence of anxiety about sex. After all, the dreams encountered by Freudian analysts and other therapists belonged to clients with neurotic problems. So there is no great contradiction here. While the relatively benign conscious, or waking, food images relevant to sex organs are usually associated with straightforward sensual pleasure, the threatening symbols that come up in dreams or nightmares are thought to emerge from repressed sexual anxieties.

At yet another concrete level, the link between food and sexuality can be seen in the widely held traditional beliefs, particularly prevalent in Asia, that certain foods and animal organs have aphrodisiac qualities. Most of these beliefs concern the enhancement of male potency. Conventional folk wisdom in the West has it that potency can be increased by eating clams, oysters, and, according to one folk saying I've heard in the U.S. Midwest, even pumpkin pie! In general, highly spiced and gourmet foods are thought to be more conducive to both male and female arousal than bland items. One study found that self-described gourmets considered themselves more sensual than other people. Some of the more bizarre-sounding sex stimulants for males are hardly food items at all, such as the now obsolete notion that injections of goat-gland extracts can perk up a reluctant penis. There is, however, still a lucrative Asian market for ground rhinoceros horns, elephant tusks, bear livers, and certain plant roots.

How people eat—ranging from delicate, slow, or picky to fast, robust, and indiscriminate—can also have direct implications for how they make love. Given all the parallel relationships between sex and food, including the familiar analogies between sexual desire and hunger (not for nothing do we speak of sexual hungers and appetites), it takes no great leap of the imagination to suggest that a person's eating style is probably very similar to his or her lovemaking style. This commonsense notion has been confirmed occasionally in conversations I have had, mainly with women colleagues. The only other evidence I have found is in clinical case histories.

Therapists who have worked with people suffering from bulimia and anorexia frequently report that these eating disorders involve the same sort of family dynamics from which sexual pathologies can result. Both are often connected with sexual abuse. Many of the adolescent girls who became anorexic were either fearful of sexual exploitation or the victims of it at an earlier age. Extreme dieting, then, may be an effort to delay sexual maturation, reducing the chances of being targeted for sexual abuse. Where the family atmosphere has been puritanical about sexual matters, the anorexic girl may be attempting to prevent maturation as a way of repressing anxieties about her own sexual arousal.

It is also possible that eating disorders rooted in sexual issues may run in the opposite direction, toward overeating rather than anorexia. Young women who have experienced sexual abuse in childhood, or rape or other sexual trauma in adulthood, may try to gain excessive weight as a defense tactic. Persuasive clinical reports indicate that such women may be consciously or unconsciously trying to defend themselves against further abuse by gaining enough weight so as to become unattractive as sexual objects. Greater weight can also be an important source of security because of the advantage it can provide when trying to fend off an attacker.

A very different food-sex connection has been identified for bulimia. The bingeing and purging are thought to arise from early experiences that leave young girls feeling deprived of attention and emotional support. They turn to food as a way of comforting themselves. But since they also wish to be sexually attractive in order to gain the emotional attentions they have missed, the same excessive eating that provides comfort is also a threatening source of guilt and frustration. Whereas the anorexic tends to be unresponsive and avoiding when it comes to sexual relationships, the bulimic is likely to seek them out and, in some instances, become as promiscuous about sex as she is about food.

Jungian analysts have theorized in greater detail about relationships between food and sexuality than have other therapists because, as more than one analyst has argued, the ways people satisfy their other appetites are closely connected with the ways they experience intimacy with others. And in a 1983 article titled "Of Cookery," the French analyst Genevieve Guy-Gillet appeals to case histories indicating similarities between a woman's cooking style and style of sexuality; both can be understood as "acts of creation." Finally, in *Wisdom of the Heart,* her book devoted to the analysis of women's dreams, Karen Signell provides a good example of the Jungian approach in the case of a woman who dreamed about women baking something "layer by layer." Interpretation of this dream emphasized that the slow process of baking referred to the alchemy of developing relationships and represented the gradual progression of courtship and intimacy the dreamer wished for.

A certain amount of food consumption is essential for sexual arousal. Case histories of anorexics and controlled studies of starvation both show that extreme food deprivation reduces or eliminates sexual desire. Survivors of the Nazi concentration camps who were on starvation diets reported having frequent detailed dreams of their favorite meals, but little or no dream experiences concerning sex. And the same thing happened among a group of American conscientious objectors during World War II, when they volunteered to participate in a study of starvation. Sexual material disappeared from their conversations and daydreams as well as from their night dreams, replaced by food and eating imagery. Food can also be antithetical to sex when it sublimates or displaces sexual desire. By deliberate overeating, one can drown the desire for sex. It seems paradoxical that both too little and too much food can have the same inhibiting effect on sexuality, but this fact lends even greater weight to arguments for the intimate connections between them.

Freudian theory is again of central importance when considering the relationship between food and aggression. Unlike sex, aggression cannot be defined as an appetite. In many instances, though, it can be understood as an emotional response to the frustration of an appetite. Aggression typically shows up during infancy, when babies will bite or otherwise show anger at nipples that fail to provide a satisfying flow of nourishment. And if, as psychoanalytic writers claim, the sensual pleasure gained at the mother's breast is the basis for adult sensuality, so too can the anger and frustration encountered at the breast be seen as the basis for subsequent aggression. Since the insights gained from his patients fitted closely with these observations, it is not difficult to see why Freud asserted a close connection between sensuality and aggression, and theorized that similar psychological processes applied to both.

A case in point is Freud's concept of sublimation. A defense mechanism whereby threatening impulses are repressed but then worked out in socially acceptable ways, sublimation applies equally well to sex and aggression. Food is often the most readily available medium for its expression. By rejecting the food provided by her parents, the anorexic teenager's behavior is a sublimation of her aggression toward them that she is unable to openly express. Conversely, a teenager's repressed anger toward his or her parents can be sublimated by overeating and gaining so much weight as to embarrass the family.

Reaction formation and *rationalization* are two other Freudian defense mechanisms whereby aggression may be expressed through food. A familiar example of the first is the mother who spoils her child with too many food treats, as a way of reacting against her repressed hostility toward the child. This sort of reaction formation can also operate among adults, as when a wife's repressed hostility toward her husband leads her to obsessively prepare his favorite foods. Such hostility is not always repressed, however. I have heard more than one woman say "jokingly" that by overfeeding her husband with his favorite foods she might hasten his demise. By contrast, the mechanism of rationalization is likely to show up in family situations where children are forced to eat things they dislike. The rationalization allowing parents to release repressed anger by punishing children if they don't eat their spinach or drink their milk is that these items are "good for them." Freudian therapists suggest that a parent who frequently justifies his or her harsh behavior in this fashion is probably someone with repressed food anxieties dating back to childhood.

Competing at the table for food treats or extra helpings is one of the more significant childhood food experiences associated with anxiety and aggressive behavior. It is often in such situations that children learn that aggressive demands and forms of self-assertion can bring gratifying results. They can also generate resentment against siblings or other family members who are more successful at satisfying their desires. And whenever food is in short supply—among adults as well as children—aggressive forms of coercion may come into play. I can vividly recall examples of this at the Boy Scout camp I attended, when the occasional bully would threaten one of the softer boys in order to get his dessert or candy bar. There are also many accounts of deadly serious anger and resentment over food among prisoners in Nazi concentration camps.

In more conventional settings, it is easy to see a number of common ways in which aggression can be expressed through food. They range from simply refusing the offer of food or drink, and thus implicitly rejecting the person or group making the offer, to outright criticism of the quality of food someone has prepared. This aspect of food behavior is so well understood in our society that it frequently produces a classic social dilemma: the guest who is not hungry but fearful of offending his or her host by not eating everything offered. Visitors to my mother's home, for example, almost required a doctor's note if they were not up to eating everything she put on the table.

Some of the most serious ways in which food may serve as an instrument of aggression are also the most obvious: prisoners who are punished by having their rations reduced, and whole populations being starved into submission during wars or revolutions. And food may be adulterated or poisoned, either as part of a rational plan to intimidate an enemy or as an unplanned side effect. The latter is presumably what happened during the Vietnam War as a consequence of the U.S. defoliation campaign. By spraying large areas of land with Agent Orange, a defoliant designed to destroy the vegetation concealing enemy positions and to prevent American supply routes from being cut off, the campaign destroyed food supplies and crops that were essential to the survival of local civilians.

Shifting back to a more personal level, almost anyone who has spent time working in restaurant kitchens usually has a story to tell about the mistreatment of food by disaffected waiters, dishwashers, or cooks. One such story that may be apocryphal has it that, during the Depression of the 1930s, a Communist kitchen worker in New York's Waldorf-Astoria Hotel harangued the cooks about class struggle, saying that they were being exploited to prepare elaborate dishes for blood-sucking capitalists.

Caught up in the need to express their revolutionary passion, the cooks gathered together over the pot of soup about to be served that evening and urinated into it. Or so the story goes. But aggression among kitchen workers is typically focused on themselves rather than their customers. The classic accounts emphasize the tantrums of temperamental chefs working under pressure, and the arguments and fights that can erupt between waiters and other kitchen staff.

As well as the many ways food may serve as an instrument of aggression, it has also been widely believed, sometimes with little or no evidence, that eating habits can increase aggressive behavior. Just as certain foods have traditionally been associated with sexual arousal, others have been thought to stimulate aggressive behavior. Meat, particularly rare steaks (the bloodier the better), has been the usual suspect. For many years, despite the absence of any firm dietary evidence, it was the main food fed to boxers training for prize fights. This association between meat and aggressive behavior clearly follows from age-old observations of the eating habits of predatory carnivores like lions and tigers. And until archaeological studies showed that most dinosaurs were herbivores, they too were thought to be aggressive meat eaters.

More recently, and with considerable supporting evidence from dietary research, foods containing large amounts of sugar and chemical additives have been thought to stimulate aggressive behavior. The generally accepted view is that high levels of sugar, preservatives, and food-coloring compounds in the bloodstream tend to make people hyperactive and emotionally brittle in ways that easily break out into aggressive or violent behavior. Probably the best-known example of this phenomenon occurred in connection with the 1978 murders of Harvey Milk and George Moscone in San Francisco. They were shot at the city hall by Danny White, a political rival. At the subsequent trial, the so-called "twinkie defense" was put forward. The defense attorney claimed that White was not fully responsible for his actions because he had for some time been consuming a diet of Twinkies (a sugary snack item) and sugary soft drinks. This had apparently impaired his ability to control his aggressive impulses. Since the defendant was convicted, the defense obviously did not work, though presumably because of his good record as a former police officer, he received a relatively light prison sentence.

An interesting variation on the theme of dietary practices and aggression occurred during World War II. Soon after the U.S. entered the war, the German propaganda ministry distributed stories claiming that American troops would not be effective in combat. This was because, since the favorite foods of young Americans were widely known to be dairy products—ice cream, milkshakes, and the like—originating from the milk of passive cows, these Americans would lack the aggressive traits needed in combat. In fact, the only significant dairy component in U.S. field rations was the cheese bar included in some of them. Most American combat rations came in the form of small cans containing prepared items such as spaghetti and meatballs, Vienna sausages, and corned beef hash. Soldiers also received an ingenious folding can opener. It was not much bigger than a thumbnail, and, in order to have it always available, many soldiers attached it to their dog tags. By contrast, central to German army field rations were blood sausage and black bread, items certainly fitting the imagery if not the reality of an aggressive, he-man diet.

To the extent that military combat rations reflect general food and taste preferences in the societies providing those rations for their armies, the form and substance of these rations carry significant psychological implications that go well beyond familiar stereotypes about "limeys" and "krauts." For the most part, they have been dull, spartan affairs, consisting largely of whatever foods were cheap, readily available, and easily stored and transported. During the revolutionary war, for example, American soldiers subsisted mainly on flour, cornmeal, rum, rice, and occasional rations of mostly spoiled beef. Fire cakes, made by mixing flour and water into something like a pancake batter and spreading it to cook on a flat stone next to an open fire, were frequently the only meals available during the hard winter General George Washington's army camped at Valley Forge.

Other noteworthy events in the history of U.S. army rations include the replacement of the rum ration with coffee and sugar in 1832, and the literal starvation of many troops during the War of 1812 because of widespread fraud by civilian food contractors. During the American Civil War, Federal soldiers received rations of bacon, beans, hardtack, and coffee, but Confederates were often forced to live off the land however they could. The Spanish-American War of 1898 saw another major food scandal when vegetables rotted in supply ships and meat packed in inadequately sterilized cans became inedible. Reforms duly followed. By 1905, the army established its first training school for cooks and bakers. It also began developing different categories of rations for men in garrison and for those on field duty. This trend of improving rations continued to such an extent that, during World Wars I and II, it was generally acknowledged that the U.S. army was the best-fed in the world.

The changes in U.S. army rations are in many ways representative of historical changes in the typical American diet, which evolved along similar lines. Food safety was a major issue in both instances, and remains so; witness current concerns with infections caused by bacteria (*E. coli*, *Salmonella*) that result from unsafe cooking practices. Both the U.S. Food and Drug Administration (FDA) and the military services continually issue warnings about this problem. In many other parts of the world, however, preoccupation with food safety is seen as a North American, particularly American, social value. Europeans often smile or sneer at American tourists who seem appalled at the ways foods are handled and displayed in open-air markets. And until the North American supermarket style of packaging crossed the Atlantic, tourists visiting from Europe used to wonder at our plastic-wrapped food items.

A unique psychological factor associated with military rations is morale. All military authorities emphasize that the morale of soldiers depends a great deal on the quality and quantity of their food. However, especially in the case of operational field rations, the military faces a dilemma. On the one hand, such rations must be processed for long-term preservation and storage, which inevitably impair tastiness; on the other hand, the rations must retain enough appeal that soldiers under stress will not have difficulty eating them. One army report estimates that, in combat conditions, soldiers are likely to consume

40 percent less food than they would otherwise, resulting in reduced morale and physical stamina. And studies of performance during World War II suggest that prolonged consumption of monotonous processed food led to loss of appetite and depression.

Even under more benign conditions, institutional food—in high schools, universities, and hospitals, as well as the military—is often a primary target of complaints. Military policies, therefore, put a high priority on maintaining "food acceptability," and civilian institutions are also moving in this direction. Reports of test programs introducing an improved cuisine and eating atmosphere in high schools have shown that the students' lunchroom behavior also improved as a result. And when similar programs have been tried in prisons notorious for bad food, violence and other discipline problems have decreased significantly. It is gradually becoming clear that, throughout society, food quality and the conditions of consumption can have major impacts on the various psychological factors we lump together under the heading of morale.

Research over the past twenty-five years has led to significant changes both to the range of foods provided to U.S. soldiers in garrison and to the development of new field rations. The contents of garrison dining-hall menus are now designed to include popular civilian items, such as hamburgers and pizza, as well as the more traditional stews, soups, and corned beef hash. The food strategy is simply to give soldiers a broad range of choices. Salad bars and breakfast bars are available, and menus are changed seasonally. The major change in field rations, however, has been replacement of canned foods with the hermetically sealed "meal ready to eat," or MRE.

According to a recent report on operational rations, the MRE has gone through many stages of development since it was first introduced. The latest version (MRE XXI) provides a range of twenty-four entrées, including grilled chicken breast, pork chow mein, beef ravioli, and chicken Tetrazzini, as well as vegetarian options. Each entrée package includes hot sauce (for many troops, especially when they have been in the field for a few days, the standard MRE seasonings seem too bland), a flameless heating tablet, and a plastic spoon, as well as various other items, such as a cracker or bread snack, peanut butter or jelly spread, candy bar, and beverage base to be mixed with water. Once the package is opened (the tough plastic wrapping on an early version I tried several years ago resisted all but the most determined knife work, perhaps another manifestation of the American concern with food safety), the contents can be warmed on the flameless heater or eaten cold. This ration has proven to be so successful in terms of its nutrient content and acceptance by soldiers that the Israeli army has adopted it to replace its rations of canned tuna, meat, and fruit.

The U.S. military has also produced several other types of field rations, designed for special situations and identified with the usual impressive acronyms. These include the GTW (go to war) ration, a version of the MRE. It consists of one of twelve entrées, wet-packed fruit, snacks, instant coffee, and a beverage base. There is also the RLW-30 (ration lightweight-30), containing dehydrated items meant to sustain troops for up to thirty days; the LRP (long range patrol) packet, with freeze-dehydrated items designed for operations of up to ten days; and two types of high-calorie rations for operations in extreme cold weather. When all else fails, soldiers may have recourse to the survival GP-I (general purpose–improved) ration, a packet of six compressed nutrient bars to be eaten over five consecutive days. Variations of the survival ration have been designed for inclusion in navy lifeboats and air force life rafts. Surprisingly, the military has even gone so far as to develop kosher and halal field-ration packets, both with ten types of entrécs, for the benefit of Orthodox Jews and Muslims.

Many of the changes in the civilian food scene over the past twenty-five years have influenced the development of military rations. The overriding theme has been the ever-expanding diversity of foods available in our society, and the military has followed suit. In addition to the MREs offering soldiers in the field a wide range of choices among entrées, the special-purpose rations reflect the trend toward designer diets. This trend is being fueled by new findings in nutrition science and ongoing biomedical research by the military. It is now well accepted, for example, that diet can enhance the performance of athletes, the particular diet depending on the sport. And it is becoming clearer all the time that specialized diets can improve the well-being of children, the elderly, and people with certain health problems. Food producers recognize this and already provide items aimed at various segments of the civilian population, just as the military provides rations designed for various operations.

It would not be difficult to argue that, contrary to the perspectives emphasized in this chapter, many of our food behaviors and preferences have little or no connection with sex or aggression but instead are simply learned adaptations to the norms and values of our society. But the fact that sensual and aggressive behaviors first emerge during infant feeding is undeniable. Anyone who has cared for infants or young children can testify to this regardless of whether they have ever heard of Freud. And on the evidence of common experience, it is also undeniable that throughout our lives, in one way or another, food is a primary medium for experiences of sensuality and manifestations of aggression. Freud's genius was to recognize the underlying deep structure of feelings and emotions associated with food that originate in infancy and persist through adulthood. If nothing else, the various adult food pathologies and eccentricities provide more than enough evidence to validate this insight. At the same time, Freud was also famous for acknowledging that there are many everyday activities, including eating, that have no hidden connections with sex or aggression but are just part of our effort to get through the day.

Military field rations are a perfect example. They have traditionally been the most commonplace items, their primary purpose to provide enough energy to keep soldiers functioning effectively in combat. Yet U.S. army rations have steadily evolved toward the relatively high standards of the current MREs. And setting aside all considerations of improved food technologies or humanitarian concerns, the apparent reason for this lies in the inescapable social and emotional significance of food. It is because adequate nutrition alone is not enough to sustain soldiers' morale, nor even enough to keep them eating when hungry, that expensive research efforts have been made to produce the wide range of MRE entrées. And it is also because of research findings emphasizing the importance of psychological factors involved in eating that MREs include the amenities of condiments and heating tablets, as well as plastic utensils. These items allow soldiers to personalize and fuss a bit over their rations in a way that can convert their moments of eating in the field into at least a minimally satisfying social occasion.

The recent developments in field rations are also noteworthy because the military research has generally been conducted according to scientific standards. There has been little contamination from the business interests (short-term profits and marketing fads) of the civilian food industry, which can change at a moment's notice. It therefore offers a relatively objective basis for understanding long-term trends in nutrition and food acceptability that may influence civilian society. In other words, just as the army jeep was a forerunner of the civilian trend toward four-wheel drive suburban utility vehicles, and the combat boot a forerunner of Doc Marten boots, military food developments may be telling of future changes to civilian foods. This is not to say that in ten or twenty years we will all be eating MREs but, rather, that some of the underlying concepts embodied in the MRE and other rations may well become influential in the civilian marketplace.

CHAPTER 7

The Road to Wellville

MANY PEOPLE THINK that any attempt to predict the future of food and eating behaviors is a futile activity— a mug's game. By all accounts, the future of food is laden with contradictions that all converge on a mug's conclusion: the future will be like the past, only more so. The "more so" follows from the holy trinity of consumer motives. Sanctified by a century of market research and known by one name or another to all professionals in the field, the holy trinity stipulates that what consumers want from food is good taste, good health, and convenience, preferably all at once. The perennial problem confronting everyone in the food business, and the source of many of the contradictions discussed in this chapter, is that at least two of the three desired food qualities have always been antithetical to one another. Cheeseburgers and fries are tasty and convenient but not healthy; fruits and vegetables are healthy and convenient but not very tasty; various pastas can be tasty and healthy but not too convenient. And so it goes. The result has always been some sort of trade-off. But it appears that such trade-offs will become less severe in the future because advances in the preparation, preservation, and distribution of food are increasing the possibility of producing items, including whole meals, that are tasty, relatively healthy, and even convenient, if one can afford the price of convenience.

Yet despite the progress under way toward fulfilling our desires to have all the pleasures and benefits that food can provide with the least amount of effort, conflicts and trade-offs persist. In their efforts to deal with this, the major players in the food industry (restaurants, supermarkets, and manufacturers) have decided to focus on the convenience issue, as it is the one that lends itself most readily to technological improvements. Although taste and health are also receiving substantial attention, these are fraught with much more long-term uncertainty. During the 1980s, for example, the food industry began to emphasize healthy meals and grocery products, only to find that, in the '90s, taste and convenience had begun to overshadow consumer concerns with health. Culture commentators generally attribute this shift to a near-irrational sense of self-indulgent well-being in our society, stimulated by the rapid economic growth and prosperity of the '90s. Be that as it may, the food industry soon realized that profits lay in the direction of improved convenience.

Market research shows an unabated public appetite for convenience foods. Increasing majorities of consumers rate shopping and cooking as dull, low-priority activities. This is particularly true of younger, unmarried people living alone or with other singles. The result is a continuing trend away from traditional home-cooked meals shared by families. Indeed, one of the few predictions that marketing experts, scholars, and culture critics of cuisine seem to agree on is that the home-cooked family meal will continue to decline in favor of several new alternatives.

Most prominent among these alternatives is the home-meal replacement, or HMR, as it is known in the food trade. The home-meal replacement has been developed quite independently from the military MRE discussed in chapter 6, but they are similar in that both are self-contained meals designed for consumer convenience. But the similarity ends at this basic level, because, unlike the traditional Chinese restaurant and delicatessen take-out items from which they evolved, HMRs come in a wide range of forms representing a broad variety of cuisines. They are also aimed at upscale, gourmet-seeking customers. Recent reports in trade magazines are unanimous in predicting that trends among first-class restaurants will include the marketing of expensive meals that may be ordered in advance, cooked to suit the customers' preferences, and then delivered hot to their doorsteps. Prospective variations on this pricey trend are said to include restaurant express outlets devoted entirely to serving customers who order a meal from an Internet menu and pick it up at a curbside window on the way home from work.

At the same time, eating outside the home is increasing. Marketing experts now estimate that 50 percent of all food dollars is being spent on eating out. And because of this growing trend, recent analyses of restaurant sales have led to the prediction that there will not be enough traditional cook-and-serve restaurants available to meet future demands. And so it is further predicted that culinary work will be modified to become a type of food-assembly operation. Extending the techniques developed in fast-food outlets, restaurant kitchens will use pre-prepared foods and preproportioned ingredients that can be assembled into meals by unskilled workers. The positive effect of this is thought to be improved quality control, cleanliness, and efficiency; the negative will probably be the dumbing-down of cuisine, as many restaurant meals become standardized products.

An interesting recent countertrend is the gourmet-sandwich shop. Sometimes referred to as providing "adult limited-service dining," these shops are designed to fill the gap between fast-food burger-pizza-taco joints that cater primarily to teenagers and young adults and sit-down restaurants or traditional diners. Designed to offer a wide variety of freshly made, prepackaged gourmet sandwiches in an efficient, no-waiting-line environment, the new shops aim to attract customers who ordinarily go to conventional deli counters, as well as those who want a change from the limited range of fast-food items. In addition to familiar deli items, designer-sandwich shops also provide innovative veggie items and wraps. Promoters of this trend suggest that these shops are now doing for the sandwich what Starbucks did for coffee.

Beyond the newly emerging sandwich shops and predicted mix of restaurants providing traditional meals, assembly-line meals, and home-meal replacements, the contradictions growing out of the public demand for convenience and tastiness are already being addressed by transformations under way in supermarkets. These are becoming ever more sophisticated outlets for ever more diversified ready-to-eat, ready-to-heat, and ready-to-cook foods. At one level, the steam-table items increasingly available in supermarkets compete directly with restaurants by allowing consumers to assemble their own personalized, ready-to-eat HMRs. But at other levels, supermarkets are providing a much greater range of convenience possibilities through their ready-to-heat and ready-to-cook products.

Sales reports show that the most popular ready-to-heat items are appetizing, reduced-fat, and vitamin-mineral fortified foods designed for popping into the microwave. In principle, this would seem to satisfy the ideal of tastiness, health, and convenience. But in practice, what this comes down to is likely nothing much more than frozen Pop-Tarts or vegetarian pizza. When it comes to convenience, however, such products are considered to be a step up from a can of pork and beans or corned beef hash. In any case, the microwave is well on its way to replacing the can opener; there has been a steady rise in the sales of frozen prepared foods at the expense of canned foods.

And this situation seems to be growing more complex. New types of ready-to-cook products are appearing that are expected to challenge the dominating ready-to-heat-and-eat items. Chief among these are gourmet, cook-it-yourself meal kits that can be prepared in thirty minutes or less. Currently being test marketed, these kits provide elaborate dinners such as filet mignon with bacon and polenta cakes, and breast of duck with pomegranate molasses glaze. Supermarkets are also expanding their range of convenient natural and organic vegetarian offerings, as an increasing number of consumers try to avoid foods treated with pesticides and chemical preservatives. In some cases, the markets are introducing special spaces—stores within stores— entirely dedicated to products such as organically grown, prewashed salads and vegetables. These are almost always described as fresh, because marketing studies report that the term "fresh" now attracts more shoppers than any other word associated with food. Also striking is the growth in the number of meat substitutes, such as soybean burgers. Not content with its hamburger substitutes, for example, Gardenburger is reported to be introducing a meatless "chicken" fillet suitable for grilling.

There is also a growing demand for what are referred to as full-taste traditional foods, those foods containing high levels of fat, such as beef steak and ice cream. Increasingly popular too are the fusion foods, such as salsa chutney, combining ingredients drawn from radically different cuisines, and an infinite variety of snack items. This last category includes all the familiar chips, dips, nuts, and crackers, as well as their newer variations: fruit chips, garlic-and-onion potato chips, and all manner of gourmet crackers. Also becoming available in this category is an automated, french-fried potato vending machine, and a line of snacks designed as "mini main meal" sandwiches that can be eaten on the run and are expected to be especially appealing to children, if not to their busy parents.

Foods with child appeal are generally predicted to become more important in the future since marketing studies show that children have an increasingly strong influence on consumer buying habits. Breakfast foods are a conspicuous example of successful child-centered product design and merchandising. And no doubt inspired by the success of fast-food marketing to children with things like Ronald McDonald playgrounds, supermarkets are beginning to provide child play areas, whereas food manufacturers are developing a new range of items with child appeal. One of the more extreme efforts reportedly under way by Heinz is a green ketchup that is being test marketed to children under the name "EZ Squirt Blastin' Green Ketchup!"

(Just the thing, perhaps, for children to put on their vending-machine french fries.)

All forecasters agree that, in the foreseeable future, super-markets will continue to offer a steadily expanding range of convenience foods, as well as the already broad range of services (laundry, dry-cleaning, photo development, video rentals, blood-pressure testing machines, prescription drugs) provided in the larger stores. This is further testimony to the overriding priority given to convenience. But before considering the psychological implications of this trend, there is another trend gaining ground in the food industry that deserves attention because it may eventually rival the importance of convenience. It takes the form of new products specifically designed to enhance health as well as of traditional foods that apparently have newly identified health-enhancing qualities. The former are often referred to in the industry as "nutraceuticals."

Nutraceuticals are loosely defined as food products that have been infused with drugs, herbs, vitamins, and minerals shown to improve energy levels, reduce emotional tensions, or protect against diseases. Examples include a vitamin-fortified drink called Power Frappucino currently being tested by Starbucks; tortilla chips containing the herb St. John's Wort, believed to counteract depression; and a sports drink called Champion Lyte that replaces the electrolytes lost through exercise but contains no sugars, fats, or carbohydrates. Many of the energy bars available in supermarkets and used as survival rations by the military are also in the nutraceutical category. Sales of such products are predicted to grow rapidly because of the positive, super-health benefits they supposedly provide. They should not be confused, however, with organically grown produce or other natural food items that merely allow consumers to avoid potentially harmful chemical preservatives.

At least one recent marketing report indicates that approximately 50 percent of American consumers believe foods have medicinal properties. This percentage will undoubtedly increase as the U.S. Food and Drug Administration (FDA) continues to publicize new research findings on the health benefits of many traditional foods. In October 2000, for example, the FDA granted Tropicana the right to claim that its orange juice can help prevent high blood pressure and stroke because it is low in sodium and high in potassium. Not to be outdone, Minute Maid is bringing out an orange juice fortified with zinc and vitamins C and E. Another company is introducing a pasta low in carbohydrates (to presumably reduce the risk of diabetes and obesity) and high in soy protein, which is believed to protect against heart disease by helping prevent the buildup of fatty deposits in blood vessels. And the October 20, 2000, edition of *Time* magazine reported in detail on research findings showing that fatty acids (omega-3 compounds) in sardines, salmon, tuna, and other fish also help prevent fatty deposits from building up to the point of blocking arteries. It seems likely that, just as soy protein is being added to various traditional foods, omega-3 acids will become an additive aimed at those people who dislike fish.

Fruits and vegetables have for a long time been known to be health enhancing because of the vitamins, minerals, and fiber they provide. But yet another recent report suggests that diets high in tomatoes and carrots can help protect against both lung cancer and prostate cancer. Even bread has attained a certain health status, since there is evidence that emotional tensions may be calmed by consuming whole-grain breads. I could keep listing the health benefits associated with familiar foods and nutraceuticals. Almost everything is good for something, and a simplistic reading would suggest that the future royal road to healthy longevity will be found in the aisles of our supermarkets. There could be a good deal of truth in this, except that the foreseeable future also contains a number of contradictory trends.

Already noted in the earlier discussion of convenience foods, the chief contradiction to the health-through-food trend is the renewed popularity of tasty, convenient, high-fat products. In other words, the royal road to good taste is paved with the animal fats that clog arteries. This is particularly true in societies like ours, where so many people are sedentary and where desires for fatty items are constantly fanned by advertising. And what could be more convenient than the Big Macs, Whoppers, fries, and shakes available almost everywhere? Thus, whereas one segment of the food industry is producing the nutraceuticals, fish, orange juice, and other items now considered health facilitators, another—and much larger—segment of the industry is busily seducing us with bigger burgers, steaks, doughnuts, and ever more bizarre gourmet ice creams. Now and in the near future, what seems to be happening is the simultaneous growth of antithetical consumption patterns. Taste allied with convenience is clearly pitted against health, but both are prospering. Both have large consumer support, and, despite the contradiction, they often overlap one another.

Much as we might like to blame the food industry for this state of affairs, the fault lies mainly with ourselves. Marketing studies show that most of us are resolutely inconsistent, going for taste and convenience one day, health the next. Or we try to split the difference between them every day. In one of the surveys conducted with my colleagues, we found that people typically indulged themselves in the tastier, fatty items during the evening. The psychology at work here is easily understood: people want variety, and the temptation to splurge with tasty, convenient foods is particularly hard to resist at the end of the day. According to clinical theories, this is the time of day when the mental energy required to inhibit our impulses is generally at its lowest point. However, marketing studies indicate other, more puzzling, contradictions. Why, for example, at a time when home cooking is on its way to becoming the exception rather than the rule, is there a boom in the sales of expensive, high-quality stoves, refrigerators, and other kitchen equipment? And why, when fewer and fewer people have either the time to cook at home or the skills to do so, are professional chef TV shows gaining popularity? The answer to the first question is apparently status. Like the newly popular mini-mansion homes, top-of-the-line kitchen appliances have become status symbols. The symbolic value of oversized stainless steel refrigerators seems to far outweigh their use value. And the intrinsic pleasure or pride of ownership gained from such objects might be called the trophy-kitchen phenomenon.

At first glance, the contradiction represented by the growing popularity of TV cooking shows seems more difficult to understand. Why should anyone who doesn't do much cooking enjoy viewing the experts who do? Perhaps the simplest answer can be found in the analogy to spectator sports: we gain a vicarious sense of accomplishment and satisfaction from watching experts do things that are far beyond our own abilities. But there must be more to it than this, because compared with golf, baseball, or football there is hardly any serious risk or tension involved when Chef Pierre cooks a soufflé. A more complex explanation may be found in psychoanalytic theory explaining how an object or activity can take on the quality of a ritual fetish: when a once commonplace activity such as cooking becomes scarce or difficult to carry out, it can acquire a new symbolic significance and may increasingly be valued as a reassuring ritual object. The gourmet cooking demonstrated by TV chefs as they perform the magic that transforms foodstuffs into delicious cuisine can become fascinating to many viewers, providing assurance that such things are possible. And so it may be precisely because the audience lacks the time and skill needed to produce culinary delights that they can experience a kind of voyeuristic satisfaction from seeing how it may be accomplished.

Another variation on the theme of food as fetish was suggested by my colleague Bob Kastenbaum in his essay on the attraction "old food" has for "fast people." This apparent contradiction in which people leading a fast, postmodern lifestyle seek out traditional foods reminiscent of the meals their grandparents enjoyed is seen by Kastenbaum as a form of "edible nostalgia." The old food in this case serves as a fetish with the power to symbolically revive feelings associated with the bygone continuities of traditional family life. Most of us can easily recognize this type of food-oriented psychodrama being acted out on holidays such as Christmas and Thanksgiving, when people gather over meals that have become part of their family history. The foods served on these occasions can carry a wide variety of emotional meanings for family members. The meal as a whole, as well as specific items on the menu, will usually evoke shared family stories, myths, and memories of long-gone relatives. In this fashion, such "old foods" may embody and help preserve significant aspects of the family culture. The traditional holiday meal, therefore, will undoubtedly persist, even though it contradicts general trends toward convenience and health.

It is just because of these trends, as well as the increasing diversity of food products available and the contradictory patterns of consumer behaviors noted earlier, that marketing forecasters anticipate profound changes in the organization of supermarkets. It is now accepted that supermarkets are already on the way to reinventing themselves as nutrition, cooking, and cuisine information centers, with computerized databases, on-line ordering facilities, and all the other apparatus of the information age. Accordingly, they will not only sell food in all its forms but also provide the various sorts of knowledge that different groups of consumers seek out as they try to make decisions in the face of bewildering diversity. This is a curious and rather ironic circular development, since the main source of consumer confusion lies in the very things supermarkets are doing in order to satisfy consumer demands. Only now, having transformed themselves into multifaceted cornucopias of foods and services, supermarkets are turning to high-tech information systems to reduce the confusion.

When viewed in a larger perspective, increasing levels of confusion and uncertainty appear to be one of the inevitable social and emotional themes associated with the future of food. The trend toward convenience, for example, has already spawned an unparalleled range of restaurant and supermarket alternatives, and there appears to be no end in sight. The cover cartoon of the November 27, 2000, edition of *The New Yorker* epitomized this point with a futuristic scene showing a man seated in front of a computer and consuming a virtual turkey dinner through a tube linking his mouth to the screen. Aside from such fantasies, the continuing proliferation of convenient products is bound to make the task of selecting from among all the alternatives more difficult and confusing. One general result of this situation is the growing number of venues, such as information-age supermarkets, websites, and TV programs, as well as traditional books and magazines, offering information and advice. And these will all surely continue to proliferate.

On the other hand, this trend may generate yet another contradiction as some consumers react to the overwhelming range of mass-produced, mass-marketed items by seeking out more personalized food experiences. The beginnings of such a countertrend can already be seen taking shape in the form of retro mom-and-pop specialty grocery stores and restaurants. These throwbacks to the 1930s and '40s are beginning to attract people who are ready to pay a premium for the comforting sense of security associated with personalized service. A noteworthy precedent suggesting that the main trend and the countertrend may both expand and prosper exists in the travel field. In this case, the dominance of convenient high-tech hotels has not prevented the growing popularity of mom-and-pop bed-and-breakfast facilities. Reaction to the flood of convenience foods is also likely to include an elitist response pattern, in which people reinvent home cooking-from-scratch as a gesture against the mass marketing of convenience. An analogous case can be seen among young women who have taken up knitting, quilting, and sewing as hobbies.

No such pattern of trend and countertrend is likely to emerge in connection with health, however. Unlike the potential demand for inconvenient "old" foods, there is no straightforward market for anti-health foods as such. Instead, there are only the more subtle temptations toward convenient, sweet, fatty products as occasional treats for when we feel we owe ourselves a little self-indulgence. Needless to say, this rationalization works well enough to support McDonald's and all the other firms selling such products. Their sales will probably go on growing side by side with increasing public concern about healthy food practices, because of the latent message out there that "eating one or two now and then won't kill you."

Assuming it continues to grow as predicted, the eating-for-health (also known as the food-as-medicine) trend carries a number of important psychological implications. Most involve a mixture of guilt feelings and feelings of moral superiority. People generally tend to feel guilty when indulging in junk food, and self-righteous when they make an effort to avoid it. The guilt aspect is already so well entrenched in our collective national psyche that we are often ready to trot out apologies or rationalizations for even thinking about eating a Big Mac or an ice cream. This is particularly true for all of us concerned about our weight. In the collective eye of our society, anyone who appears significantly overweight tends to be judged as a self-indulgent consumer of too many unhealthy foods. Rightly or wrongly, this prevalent moralistic view is applied to, and accepted by, almost everyone (Julia Child is a conspicuous exception), including former U.S. president Clinton, who is well known for his acknowledged inability to resist Big Mac attacks. It is the near-universal sense of guilt over the consumption of unhealthy but delicious foods that has generated songs like "Junk Food Junkie" and jokes about a junk-food prohibition law similar to the alcohol prohibition of the 1920s. It is also responsible for generating a great deal of research by food corporations aimed at developing healthy versions of delicious foods. If we never see a healthy burger, fries, or milkshake that tastes the same as the unhealthy original, it won't be because the food companies are not trying their best to create them.

The other end of the psychological spectrum concerning the health value of food is defined by self-righteous feelings of moral superiority. There is hardly anyone in our society who does not at some point innocently enjoy the pleasures of tasty unhealthy items. Those who are able to master their appetites and follow the generic healthy diet (mostly grains, vegetables, and fruit, with little animal fat, sugar, or salt) often behave like religious converts. It is clearly yet another paradox of our modern age that, at a time when a historically unparalleled array of tasty and convenient foods is available, the recommended healthy diet is reminiscent of the items consumed in a premodern monastery.

But the daily eating habits of most people, so long as they are not seriously obese, ill, or given to quasi-religious ascetic values, are not closely connected with extreme feelings of either guilt or moral superiority. Instead, they tend to oscillate somewhere in the middle or swing back and forth between such feelings. Depending on their personal and social circumstances, most people cycle between these emotions or remain indifferent to them. This may very well change in the future because preventive public health campaigns seem destined to intensify and become more effective. (Even as I write, one of my colleagues has received a large government grant to develop personalized messages—personalized in that they address, for example, the immediate social benefits for teenagers of not smoking, rather than the long-term health issues—for use in public health campaigns. This sort of work is also going on at many other universities.) It appears inevitable that, driven by the accelerating costs of medical care, preventive health efforts emphasizing dietary discipline and restraint are bound to increase. Anti-smoking campaigns have already established a precedent for making personal consumption behaviors a matter of public policy. We may never see outright prohibition of cigarettes, but we may see warning labels on double cheeseburgers.

Quite apart from speculations based on present knowledge of the health implications of food, the future may also bring unexpected changes as a consequence of research findings. One plausible scenario follows from the genome project, which will soon allow the genetic characteristics determining our metabolic rates and vulnerability to various allergies, diseases, and other health problems to be identified. This is becoming possible at the same time as we are learning much more about the health effects of different foods. At some point in the future, these developments will probably converge. The result is likely to be that, once people have their genetic profiles, they will be able to enter them in a computer that can compile the ideal diet for that profile. We may then know exactly what the experts think we ought to eat to maximize our health and longevity. Remote as it may be, and despite its obvious benefits, the psychological effects of such a situation are a bit daunting, because it would further rationalize consumption, reducing or eliminating all the pleasures we can now enjoy from impulsive, alfresco eating. If one were writing science fiction, the next logical step would be a computer-chip implant that would automatically make us ill at the thought of eating a disapproved item!

In certain respects, the brave new world of tailor-made diets is already here. Many people with food allergies must avoid certain foods, as do those with heart disease, diabetes, and other ailments. And we all have a primitive, experience-based system for matching our eating habits to our genetically determined physiology. While growing up, we gain a fair sense of what foods disagree with us and so learn to avoid these items. And, in addition to following diets based on common sense and medical advice, people are attracted to the more extreme eating programs that promise to improve their looks, intelligence, and stress-coping ability. Among these, one that stands out because of its stark simplicity is fasting.

In Western European culture, there is an ascetic fasting tradition that dates back at least to the biblical prophets. Such fasting is believed to aid spiritual development. When combined with intensive prayer or meditation, going with little or no food for several days is almost guaranteed to bring on visionary or out-of-body experiences. Fasting has also been an important feature of the Native American vision quest tradition, and in Asia it is central to the yogic path toward mind–body unity. Such fasting practices generally provide an effective, low-tech psychophysiological means of attaining altered states of consciousness. When practiced mainly for health, however, fasting is usually limited to a routine in which liquid nutrients only are consumed for two or three days, until the person's system is "cleaned out."

An extreme variation on the theme of fasting is breatharianism. As expounded by Wiley Brooks in *Breatharianism: Breathe and Live Forever*, this practice maintains that eating is a major threat to health. Instead, air and light can provide all the energy necessary to sustain human life. Brooks claims to have lived for twenty years without eating. Other books along this line, such as Jasmuheen's *Living on Light* and Morris Krok's *Diet, Health, and Living on Air*, emphasize starting out slowly in the practice of breatharianism with deep breathing exercises, a yogic technique that can do no harm and may have important benefits. Whether anyone can live very long on air and light remains to be seen, since no substantial evidence for this claim is available.

There is, on the other hand, a growing body of human and animal research suggesting that a 20 to 30 percent reduction in the number of calories consumed by most people in our society would bring dramatic improvements in health and longevity. One recent review concluded that rapid increases in the availability of tempting foods in industrialized countries over the past few decades have led to levels of consumption that clearly pose a threat to the health and longevity of most consumers. Is it at all conceivable that such evidence will mount to the point of convincing significant numbers of people to adopt quasi-anorexic diets? Hardly. But then none of us who came of age fifty years ago watching Humphrey Bogart movies would have imagined a time when we would consider cigarettes poisonous, wear safety belts in cars, and read nutrition labels in supermarkets. So it is possible that the ever-expanding knowledge and technologies influencing how we think about food may bring greater surprises than those we have seen up to now.

In the meantime, the current and future trends discussed in this chapter should be enough to convince anyone that the complexity and pluralism of our food environment will continue to grow. And that the psychological meanings of food will become more ambiguous, as we all will have greater opportunities to indulge our particular preferences. Part of this ambiguity will follow from the difficulty of sorting through the great range of possibilities in order simply to discover our own preferences. And at least three specific behavioral consequences seem likely. The first and most probable will be a rise in the incidence of eating disorders and neurotic food fetishes. A large amount of social science research shows that, when the traditional values and norms governing behavior begin to break down in the face of confusing or contradictory new possibilities, people often react by adopting arbitrary, superstitious beliefs. Eating disorders fit this generalization very neatly since they mainly occur among young people who are notoriously susceptible to arbitrary, magical notions and who grow up in environments where food is plentiful. In addition to clear cases of bulimia and anorexia, it is likely that more people will develop rigid food preferences and compulsive eating habits as a defense against the chaotic food atmosphere.

Second, a much higher degree of social class segmentation is likely to become characteristic of eating habits. Those who are relatively well-off and well educated will be in the best position to take advantage of information that helps them make optimum choices from among a huge range of more or less tasty, healthy, and convenient items. Countless studies have shown that the ability to delay gratification, ward off seductive advertising, and resist temptations of immediate sensory pleasures are all associated with higher levels of education. And it is well known that this pattern carries over to eating behaviors. As the food environment becomes more complex, then, social class segmentation can be expected to become even more pronounced. And the present tendency toward obesity, health problems, and a shorter life span among the very poor will probably increase despite the efforts of government and private health organizations to counteract this. Throughout the 20th century, well-intentioned programs designed to improve eating habits among the poor usually failed.

Finally, it seems safe to predict that the complex food environment of the future will become the arena for an increasingly intense battle between contemporary counterparts of Stoics (advocates of ascetic health) and Dionysians (advocates of pleasure and convenience). Both sides, and some in the middle claiming to represent the best of both worlds, will spin persuasive arguments and mount campaigns to manipulate public opinion. The chief result will most likely be to raise the level of public confusion.

Trying to forecast the future of anything as variable and complicated as food and eating behaviors has already been acknowledged as a mug's game. But even if the predictions suggested here should turn out to be wrong, the value of the exercise lies in how much it reveals about the limitations of our present knowledge. Although general trends in the marketplace are clearly observable, there are also clear countertrends and contradictions that make predictions based on present knowledge an interesting but risky gamble. Worse yet, when it comes to the future, history shows that the one thing we can most confidently predict is the occurrence of unpredictable events. Such events can profoundly change not only the foreseeable future but also our understanding of the past and present.

When I was a teenager, we had the promise of abundant clean energy from nuclear power plants. This vanished with the events at Three Mile Island and Chernobyl. Later on, when birth control pills became available, it was widely believed that we had finally entered the promised land of sexual freedom. That changed with the arrival of AIDS. Today it appears that, at least in North America and Western Europe, we are on the threshold of a new era of tasty, healthy, and convenient foods, where the only problem will be choosing among them. And yet seemingly out of nowhere, we now have lurking in the background the threat of mad cow disease, something that could conceivably worsen to the point of driving us all toward vegetarianism. Then, too, there is an ongoing debate among scientists about danger to our food systems if the genetic engineering of basic crop seeds should take a wrong turn. The future of food is not something to be taken too much for granted.

Troubling as these negative scenarios may be (I have noted only the top two; several others could keep you awake nights if you are so inclined), there is a bright side to the fact that the complexity of our food systems does not allow easy predictability. It has become widely accepted in the scientific community that a certain degree of unpredictability and uncertainty is intrinsic to complex systems, essential to their self-organization and, more importantly, to their creative reorganization. Instability, in other words, is a precondition for creative transformations. When considered from this perspective, the things we think of as disasters can also be seen as having adaptive, redemptive consequences.

Three Mile Island and Chernobyl, for example, provided clear warnings of the likelihood of even worse catastrophes and inspired greater efforts to develop renewable, nonpolluting sources of energy. AIDS generated new concern with public health issues and research findings that have significant implications for dealing with other illnesses. Mad cow disease has already encouraged many Europeans to adopt healthier diets and could have the same effect elsewhere. And potential threats to our food sources from the production of genetically modified crop seeds have stimulated public awareness and research that may enhance our understanding of ecological issues. None of this is meant to suggest that disasters are desirable. It is only to warn again that, although the speculations presented in this chapter about the future of food and changes in its psychological meanings all seem plausible at the moment, the only thing we can be sure of is that there is no free lunch.

CHAPTER 8

Concluding Reflections

ANYONE LOOKING THROUGH the diverse range of biological, historical, and social-psychological material in each of the previous chapters should have no difficulty understanding why it is impossible to organize all the factors influencing how we eat within a single framework. As noted in the introduction, the more one learns about food behaviors, the clearer it becomes that no such systematic scheme is feasible. The plain fact is that the meanings of food are disorderly and that human appetites are anarchic. Furthermore, our appetites are never far removed from our anxieties. Pushed by appetite, we worry either about getting enough to eat or about eating too much, and in between there is usually some concern about the quality of what we are eating. Thus, our thoughts and feelings about eating intermingle and overlap, and while some order can be imposed for the sake of narrative convenience, let alone coherence, it is appropriate to stay pretty loose while working through such material.

However, this does not mean it's necessary to abandon all efforts at systematic discussion. The idea that most of our food behaviors are generally guided by implicit ideologies of hedonism, nutritionism, and, to a lesser degree, the religious and moral values I've called spiritualism is a broadly descriptive theme that can be useful when trying to sort out the factors underlying individual food preferences. Nor do I think it is a mere coincidence that these ideologies are closely parallel to the id, ego, and superego dimensions of Freud's personality theory. The parallel seems entirely suitable since virtually everything we know about human development suggests that our food behaviors are closely tied to our sense of personal identity and social-adjustment habits. The ideologies theme also helps explain why every distinctive social group has a food culture it considers superior to all others.

But at the most fundamental level, the one overriding conclusion I have reached concerns the importance of self-awareness about food. As I noted in the introduction, most of us go through life taking food for granted unless something goes wrong and a medical problem focuses our attention, or goes right and we come to appreciate some of the deeper significance of giving thoughtful attention to food. But even among those who for one reason or another begin to take food seriously, most do so in a relatively uncritical fashion. Some, probably the majority, see food only through the lenses of their desires, as a source of pleasure. Their approach to food is limited to getting the best and the most they can with the least expenditure of time, energy, or money. They tend to fit the category "gourmand" rather than "gourmet." In the latter category are those who make efforts to acquire substantial knowledge about food and cuisine, primarily to use it to gain social status—to "win friends and influence people." For them, the ability to recommend excellent, inexpensive restaurants, or to prepare ("whip up!") a tasty omelette or pasta dish for friends, colleagues, or potential lovers, is a valuable form of social capital that usually brings good returns. And then, at the top of the social-capital heap, as it were, there are the gourmet-food devotees who pride themselves on organizing meals, usually dinner parties, the way Hollywood producers organize films. They lavish careful, even obsessive, attention on the menu (script), on atmosphere, decor, and tableware (the set), and on inviting the correct mix of guests (the cast). The dinner party itself becomes a type of performance art, which afterward can serve as a choice item of gossip for all concerned.

A related category of people who take food seriously consists of those who do so primarily out of a narcissistic preoccupation with their bodies. They tend to believe with a vengeance that you are what you eat, and so become immersed in health-food lore, diets, and nutrient supplements. In this case, the apparently serious focus on food may be little more than a neurotic defense mechanism arising from obsessive fears of the effects of aging and disease. When looking beneath the conventional masks of many people who show a palpable concern with food, what one sees all too often is an orientation that is essentially exploitative: food as a means to some end, rather than an end in itself.

But the point here is not simply to criticize people for not having a more thoughtful attitude toward food and failing to appreciate its profound significance. Indeed, why should anyone care about food except as something that can provide pleasure and maintain health in the most convenient ways possible? And why should we not try to make the most of this while we can, since, in the end, if we live long enough, our health will fail, our taste sensitivities will fade, and convenience will hardly matter?

What matters a great deal, however, is our consciousness of self in daily life. Self-awareness is the foundation for our sense of consciousness, and the act of eating, of choosing what to put in our bodies, is the most fundamental way in which we enact and experience self-awareness. Without eating, there is no being. And with eating comes the most basic, inescapable experience of self-awareness that shapes our consciousness of self and the world around us. "You are what you eat." "The way to a man's heart is through his stomach." As well as anything else can, such aphorisms convey the idea I wish to emphasize: that eating and the social-aesthetic atmosphere that goes with it are what basically determine positive or negative self-awareness. And it is self-awareness that furnishes the larger interior of con-sciousness.

All of this is already well started during infancy and early childhood, where the direct connections between eating and rudimentary self-awareness, in the form of social-emotional reactions to feeding, are clearly visible. More significantly, early childhood is also the time when displays of food preferences indicate that *critical* self-awareness is beginning to emerge. That is, self-awareness is on its way to becoming critical the moment children start sniffing and tasting food and then acting out their judgment of it as good or bad, or maybe in-between.

The importance of such critical self-awareness can hardly be exaggerated. Without it, there can be little or no basis for us as children to begin to experience personal autonomy. Nor, as teenagers or adults, to experience the extent to which our existential condition—our being in the world—is shaped by how we choose to manage the relationship between our biological and our social-psychological needs. To put it concretely, I am suggesting that critical self-awareness about food relates in fundamental ways to central issues of personal meaning in the life course of any person. From childhood onward, our ability to control what we eat, or whether we eat at all, is the single, most basic aspect of life in which we have full power to assert autonomy. When a young child refuses food, or spits out something disliked, he or she is taking a first important step toward self-determination. Viewed in this philosophical light, every child's highchair can be seen as the site of a small-scale struggle for existential freedom.

It must be acknowledged, of course, that from infancy through the end of childhood we are all encouraged and conditioned to accept the foods available. There are only a few minimal alternatives to eating in conformity with the norms of our family and the larger society. But with the arrival of adolescence, if not sooner, conscious control over the foods we eat increases rapidly. At the same time, our teenage years are the period of a burgeoning sense of self-awareness. It is no accident that novel food preferences emerge along with the other experiments and innovations of this age. Teenagers' rebellions against the dietary habits of their parents may seem to be no more than a shift from conformity with their family to conformity with their peer group. Yet regardless of whether or not such rebellions are because of peer pressure, they serve important developmental functions. A robust assertion of autonomy about food enlarges the basis that is needed to form a mature sense of independent identity and critical self-awareness. This is because, having first been able to resist food conformity with the family, we are better able to later resist such conformity with our peers and, potentially, with larger segments of society. Critical self-awareness about food, therefore, can provide a developmental springboard from which to expand one's sense of autonomy into other areas of one's life.

Since our being ultimately depends on the food we eat— this is an essential aspect of everyday life—if we can attain a significant degree of critical self-awareness about our food behaviors, we are more likely to attain a deeper consciousness of self, one informed by independence or creative self-assertion. On the other hand, if we are unable to break from conformity with the consumption patterns of our society or immediate social group over something as personal as our food behavior, it seems unlikely that we could do so in other, less personal, areas of life. Thus, the developmental pathway to an enhanced consciousness of existential freedom begins or is closely associated with critical self-awareness about food.

When approached from the standpoint of developmental psychology, as outlined above, the argument that food behaviors are significant in the establishment of an independent adult consciousness rests on the importance of feeding experiences during infancy and childhood. If this seems arbitrary, there is another very different approach to the argument that can be made based on common observations of changes in adult food behaviors. In these cases, what can be seen is a directly opposite causal pattern: instead of critical self-awareness about food leading to a more independent consciousness of self, it is a changed consciousness of self that leads to critical self-awareness about food.

An example can be seen in the way many people react to major losses or traumas, such as divorce or the death of a child or spouse. Such experiences frequently bring on painful periods of self-reflection. The result of this can be a new, more thoughtful consciousness of one's condition in the world, as well as changes in one's lifestyle, including new food behaviors. Similar examples of the connection between adult consciousness and critical self-awareness about eating behaviors can be seen among people who take up serious body–mind practices, such as distance running or walking, yoga, and meditation. They often report spontaneous changes in their food preferences. These apparently are due to their enhanced attention to body–mind sensations. And there are many people who develop critical self-awareness about food after being warned to change their eating habits because of a major medical problem, such as heart disease. This sort of change may at first be adopted as a narrowly narcissistic response to the health problem but can later grow into a profound appreciation of the social and emotional significance of eating behaviors. In short, critical self-awareness about food can occur either in the natural course of development from infancy through adulthood or as a consequence of intense adult social-emotional experiences that lead to major lifestyle changes. In both cases, such critical self-awareness will be intimately bound up with the person's broader consciousness of self.

Finally, having emphasized a relatively abstract theoretical case for the importance of critical self-awareness, it seems appropriate to mention how it may apply to what might be the biggest problem of everyday food behavior: how to deal with conflicts between the holy trinity of our desires for pleasure, health, and convenience. It is a problem rooted in the meanings we attach to eating. As long as those meanings remain primarily tied to the satisfaction of our desires, there can be no end to the conflicts between them. The conflicts can be transcended, however, when our desires are tamed or relegated to a background status by placing them in a larger context of critical self-awareness. This can be accomplished only by thinking through the meanings we attach to food and realizing that they ultimately are based on, and define, our ways of being in the world. Indeed, there is a good deal to be said for the idea that we need to look beneath the conveniences of our current food systems, which we take for granted, and reclaim some of the perspectives that dictated the lives of our less civilized ancestors—namely, that eating is simultaneously the most mundane, sublime, and potentially hazardous connection we have with nature. We take our life and well-being in our hands every time we do it.

Sources

Amato, J. *The Great Jerusalem Artichoke Circus.* Minneapolis: University of Minnesota Press, 1993.

Ambrose, S. *Undaunted Courage: Meriwether Lewis, Thomas Jefferson, and the Opening of the American West.* New York: Touchstone, 1996.

Angulo, J. "Ideology and Foodways." Diss. Kansas State University, 1985.

Aron, J. "The Art of Using Leftovers: Paris, 1850–1900." *Food and Drink in History: Selections from the Annales.* Ed. R. Forster and O. Ranum. Baltimore: Johns Hopkins University Press, 1979. 98–108.

Azar, B. "What Predicts Which Foods We Eat?" *APA Monitor* Jan. 1998: 12–13.

Baerveldt, C., and P. Voestermans. "The Body as a Selfing Device: The Case of Anorexia Nervosa." *Theory and Psychology* 6.4 (1996): 693–713.

Baker, R. Introduction. *Tassajara Cooking.* By E. Brown. Berkeley: Shambhala, 1973. 1.

Barthes, R. "Toward a Psychosociology of Contemporary Food Consumption." *Food and Drink in History: Selections from the Annales.* Ed. R. Forster and O. Ranum. Baltimore: Johns Hopkins University Press, 1979. 166–73.

Beardsworth, A., and T. Keil. *Sociology on the Menu: An Invitation to the Study of Food and Society.* London: Routledge, 1997.

Becker, E. *The Denial of Death.* New York: Free Press, 1973.

Bierce, A. *The Devil's Dictionary.* 1911. New York: T.Y. Crowell, 1979.

Birch, L.L., and J.A. Fisher. "The Role of Experience in the Development of Children's Eating Behavior." *Why We Eat What We Eat: The Psychology of Eating*. Ed. E. Capaldi. Washington, DC: APA, 1996. 113–41.

Booth, D.A. *Psychology of Nutrition*. Bristol, PA: Taylor and Francis, 1994.

Brickman, P., and D.T. Campbell. "Hedonic Relativism and Planning the Good Society." *Adaptation-Level Theory: A Symposium*. Ed. M.H. Apley. New York: Academic Press, 1971. 287–302.

Brooks, W. *Breatharianism: Breathe and Live Forever*. Beryl, UT: Breatharian Institute, n.d.

Brownell, K.D., and J. Rodin. "The Dieting Maelstrom:Is it Possible and Advisable to Lose Weight?" *American Psychologist*. 49.9 (1994): 781–91.

Bruch, H. *Eating Disorders: Obesity, Anorexia, and the Person Within*. New York: Basic Books, 1973.

——. *The Golden Cage: The Enigma of Anorexia Nervosa*. Cambridge: Harvard University Press, 1978.

Burgoyne, J., and D. Clarke. "You Are What You Eat: Food and Family Reconstitution." *The Sociology of Food and Eating*. Ed. A. Murcott. Aldershot, Hants: Gower Publishing, 1983. 152–63.

Burros, Marion. "A Casserole Cooked on Top of the Stove." *New York Times*, 4 May 1994: C4.

Cash, T.F., B.A. Winstead, and L.H. Janda. "The Great American Shape-Up." *Psychology Today* 20 Apr. 1986: 30–37.

Craig, William. *Enemy at the Gates: The Battle for Stalingrad*. New York: Ballantine Books, 1973.

Davies, C. *Ethnic Humor around the World*. Bloomington: Indiana University Press, 1990.

Dichter, E. *Handbook of Consumer Motivations*. New York: McGraw Hill, 1964.

Dickson, P. *Chow: A Cook's Tour of Military Food*. New York: New American Library, 1978.

Dishman, R.K. "Compliance/Adherence in Health-Related Exercise." *Health Psychology* 1 (1982): 237–67.

Dixon, N.F. *Our Own Worst Enemy*. London: Jonathan Cape, 1987. 77–78.

Edwards, J.S.A. "Food Service/Catering: Restaurant and Institutional Perspectives of the Meal." *Dimensions of the Meal.* Ed. H. Meiselman. Gaithersberg, MD: Aspen Publishers, 2000. 223–44.

Eliade, M. *The Sacred and the Profane: The Nature of Religion.* New York: Harcourt Brace, and World, 1959.

Elias, N. *The History of Manners.* 1939. New York: Urizen Books, 1978.

Faust, J.M. "Nutrition and the Fat Cell." *International Journal of Obesity* 4 (1980): 314–21.

Fisher, M.F.K. *The Art of Eating.* 1954. New York: Vintage Books, 1976.

French, S.A., and R.W. Jeffery, "Consequences of Dieting to Lose Weight: Effects on Physical and Mental Health." *Health Psychology.* 13.3 (1994): 195–212.

Fussell, P. *Class: A Guide through the American Status System.* New York: Ballantine Books, 1983.

Gandhi, M.K. *Autobiography: The Story of My Experiments with Truth.* New York: Dover Publications, 1983.

Gergen, K. "The Social Constructionist Movement in Modern Psychology." *American Psychologist* 40 (1985): 266–75.

Goody, J. *Cooking, Cuisine and Class: A Study in Comparative Sociology.* New York: Cambridge University Press, 1982.

Gordon, R.A. *Anorexia and Bulimia: Anatomy of a Social Epidemic.* Cambridge, MA: Basil Blackwell, 1990.

Guy-Gillet, G. "Of Cookery." *Money, Food, Drink, and Fashion and Analytic Training: Depth Dimensions of Physical Existence.* Ed. J. Beebe. Fellbach Oeffingen: Verlag Adolf Bonz, 1983. 71–81.

Hessler, P. "Postcard from China: A Rat in My Soup." *New Yorker* 24 July 2000: 38–41.

Jasmuheen. *Living on Light.* San Diego: Natures First Law, n.d.

Kastenbaum, R. "Old Food for Fast People." *American Behavioral Scientist* 32.1 (1988): 50–60.

Kirk, D., and E.K. Eliason. *Food and People.* San Francisco: Boyd and Fraser Publishing, 1982.

Krok, M. *Diet, Health, and Living on Air.* San Diego: Natures First Law, n.d.

Lappe, F.M. *Diet for a Small Planet.* New York: Ballantine Books, 1975.

Levenstein, H. *Paradox of Plenty: A Social History of Eating in America*. New York: Oxford University Press, 1993.

Levi, P. *Survival in Auschwitz*. 1961. New York: Collier, 1976.

Lévi-Strauss, C. *The Raw and the Cooked*. New York: Harper and Row, 1969.

Levy, A.S., and A.W. Heaton. "Weight Control Practices of U.S. Adults Trying to Lose Weight." *Annals of Internal Medicine* 119 (1993): 661–66.

Lewin, K. "Forces behind Food Habits and Methods of Change." *The Problem of Changing Food Habits*. Bulletin 108. Washington, DC: National Research Council, 1943. 35–65.

Logue, A.W. *The Psychology of Eating and Drinking*. New York: W.H. Freeman and Company, 1986.

Martin, J.E., and P.M. Dubbert. "Adherence to Exercise." *Exercise and Sports Sciences Review*. Ed. R.L. Terjung. Vol. 13. New York: Macmillan, 1985.

Mason, V.C., A.I. Meyer, and M.V. Klicka. *Summary of Operational Rations*. U.S. Army Technical Report TR-82/013. Natick, MA: U.S. Department of Defense, 1982.

Mehrabian, A. *Basic Dimensions for a General Psychological Theory: Implications for Personality, Social, Environmental, and Developmental Studies*. Cambridge, MA: Oelgeschlager, Gunn & Hain, 1980.

Mennella, J.A., and G.K. Beauchamp. "The Early Development of Human Flavor Preferences." *Why We Eat What We Eat: The Psychology of Eating*. Ed. E. Capaldi. Washington, DC: APA, 1996. 83–105.

Mintz, S.W. *Tasting Food, Tasting Freedom: Excursions into Eating, Culture, and the Past*. Boston: Beacon Press, 1996.

Ohsawa Foundation. *Zen Macrobiotics*. Los Angeles: Ignoramus Press, 1966.

Palazolli, M.S. "The Anorexic Process in the Family." *Family Process* 27 (1986): 129–48.

Parkman, F. *The Oregon Trail*. 1849. New York: Bantam Books, 1966. 87–88.

Peters, G., L. Rappoport, L. Huff-Corzine, C. Nelson, and R. Downey. "Food Preferences in Daily Life: Cognitive, Affective and Social Predictors." *Ecology of Food and Nutrition* 33 (1995): 215–28.

Pinel, J.P.J., S. Assanand, and D.R. Lehman. "Hunger, Eating, and Ill Health." *American Psychologist* 55.10 (2000): 1105–16.

Prigogine, I., and I. Stengers. *Order out of Chaos.* New York: Bantam Books, 1984.

Rappoport, L. "Failures before Food: Psychosocial Approaches to Eating Behavior." *Recent Trends in Theoretical Psychology.* Ed. I. Lubek, R. Van Heyewijk, G. Pheterson, and C. Tolman. Vol. 4. New York: Springer Publishing, 1995. 112–18.

——. "Psychosocial and Philosophical Problematics of Foodways." *Theoretical and Philosophical Psychology* 7 (1987): 18–24.

Rappoport, L., and G. Peters. "Aging and the Psychosocial Problematics of Food." *American Behavioral Scientist* 32 (1988): 31–40.

Rappoport, L., G. Peters, L. Huff-Corzine, and R. Downey. "Reasons for Eating: An Exploratory Cognitive Analysis." *Ecology of Food and Nutrition* 28 (1992): 171–89.

Rappoport, L., G. Peters, L. Huff-Corzine, R. Downey, and T. McCann. "Gender and Age Differences in Food Cognition." *Appetite* 20 (1993): 33–52.

Richman, P. "Savoring Lunch in the Slow Lane." *Washington Post* 2 Dec. 1998: C3.

Rodin, J., and P. Salovey. "Health Psychology." *Annual Review of Psychology* 40 (1989): 533–79.

Saddalla, E., and J. Buroughs. "Profiles in Eating: Sexy Vegetarians and Other Diet Based Social Stereotypes." *Psychology Today* 15 Oct. 1981: 51–59.

Signell, K. *Wisdom of the Heart.* New York: Bantam Books, 1990.

Sloan, A.E. "Food Industry Forecast: Consumer Trends to 2020 and Beyond." *Food Technology* 52.1 (1998): 37–44.

Sokolov, R.A. *Fading Feast: A Compendium of Disappearing American Regional Foods.* New York: Farrar, Strauss and Giroux, 1981.

Tannahill, R. *Food in History.* New York: Stein and Day, 1973.

Willeford, W. "Festival, Communion, and Mutuality." *Journal of Analytical Psychology* 26 (1981): 345–55.

Index